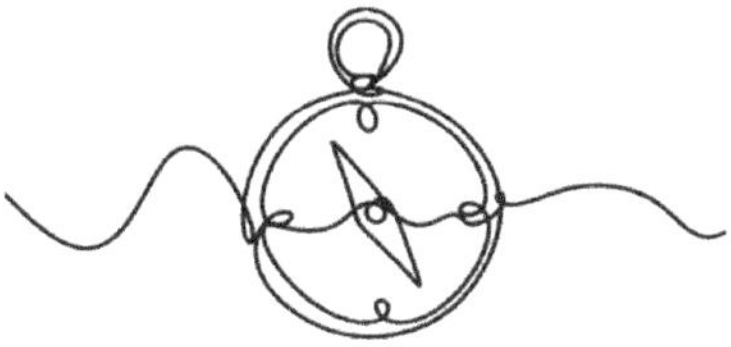

The Wanderlust Family

A Guide to Traveling with your School Age Kids

Dedication:

To all the school age kids (my own and my former students) who have taught me the beauty of opening your eyes to the world around you. I am forever grateful.

Table of Contents

Author's Note

Dear Readers,

Welcome to the second installment of our travel guide series, specially crafted for families embarking on exciting adventures with school-age kids. As a lifelong traveler, mother, and educator, it brings me immense joy to share my experiences and insights with you, drawing upon the transformative power of travel on children as they navigate the world.

Having explored various corners of the globe with my own children, I am a firm believer in the profound impact that travel can have on young minds. The first book in this series laid the foundation for traveling with infants and toddlers, highlighting the unique joys and challenges of those early years. Now, in this second guide, we will delve into the realm of school-age children, capturing the magic and opportunities that unfold as their curiosity and understanding blossom.

Traveling with school-age kids brings an exciting blend of discovery, education, and family bonding. It allows children to expand their horizons, embrace diverse cultures, and develop a sense of global citizenship. Beyond the classroom walls, children have the chance to witness history, engage with new languages, savor different cuisines, and be inspired by awe-inspiring natural wonders. These experiences help shape their perspectives, nurture empathy, and foster a lifelong love for learning.

In this guide, we will dive into practical advice and invaluable tips that cater specifically to families with school-age children. From planning itineraries that strike the perfect balance between education and fun to maximizing cultural immersion opportunities, we will explore ways to create unforgettable memories that leave lasting impressions on young hearts and minds.

Remember, this guide is not meant to be prescriptive or exhaustive. Rather, it is a compass to navigate the vast sea of possibilities that family travel presents. Each family is unique, and your journeys will be as well. Let this book serve as a trusted companion, offering suggestions, sparking ideas, and providing a roadmap to help you design the most enriching and rewarding adventures for your family.

I would like to express my deepest gratitude to all the families who have shared their stories and experiences, and to the educators and experts who have generously contributed their insights to this guide. Your wisdom and passion have shaped this book and made it a true labor of love.

May this guide inspire you to embark on incredible journeys, forge unforgettable connections, and witness the world through the eyes of your children. May it remind us all that travel is not just about the destinations we reach, but also about the transformative journey we take within ourselves and with our loved ones.

Wishing you safe travels and magical experiences!

Warmest regards,

Alice

Lifelong Traveler, Mother, and Educator

Chapter 1

The Power of Travel and Exploration: Unleashing the Potential of School-Age Children

"Travel far, travel wide, travel deep. Embrace the world and let it shape your child's mind." This quote captures the essence of why travel and exploration are such transformative experiences for school-age children. As parents, we strive to provide our children with a well-rounded education, equipping them with knowledge, skills, and values that will guide them throughout their lives. While the classroom offers a structured environment for learning, there is a world beyond those four walls that holds invaluable lessons waiting to be discovered. In this travel guide, we embark on a journey to explore the world with our kids, recognizing the immense importance and benefits of travel and exploration for their holistic development.

Expanding Horizons:

Education is not confined to textbooks and exams. By exposing children to diverse cultures, landscapes, and people, travel broadens their horizons and nurtures a sense of curiosity about the world. It dismantles stereotypes, fosters empathy, and cultivates an appreciation for the rich tapestry of humanity. As children witness different ways of life, they develop a global perspective, transcending boundaries and embracing diversity. They become more open-minded, adaptable, and better equipped to navigate the complexities of our interconnected world.

Hands-on Learning:

Travel presents an immersive and hands-on learning experience that goes beyond the theoretical knowledge imparted in classrooms. Whether it's exploring ancient ruins, observing wildlife in their natural habitats, or tasting local cuisine, every moment is an opportunity for discovery. Children engage their senses, sparking their innate curiosity and making connections between what they learn in school and the real world. Historical sites become living classrooms, museums transform into interactive exhibitions, and everyday interactions become valuable lessons in communication, problem-solving, and cultural understanding.

Stimulating Creativity:

New environments and unfamiliar surroundings awaken the imagination of school-age children. As they encounter stunning landscapes, vibrant markets, and awe-inspiring architecture, their creative juices flow. They find inspiration in the beauty and diversity of the world, leading to artistic expression through painting, writing, or photography. Travel encourages them to think outside the box, to embrace novel experiences, and to see the world through a lens of wonder. It instills a sense of adventure and a desire to explore and create, nurturing their artistic talents and allowing them to discover their passions.

Building Resilience:

Travel is not always smooth sailing. It presents challenges, unexpected situations, and moments of discomfort. However, it is precisely these obstacles that build resilience in school-age children. As they navigate unfamiliar environments, adapt to different cultures, and overcome language barriers, they develop problem-solving skills, self-confidence, and the ability to thrive outside their comfort zones. They learn to be flexible, patient, and resilient in the face of adversity—a valuable skill set that will serve them throughout their lives.

Strengthening Family Bonds:

Family travel creates lifelong memories and strengthens the bonds between parents and children. It offers an opportunity for quality time, away from the distractions of daily routines, where shared experiences and adventures become the foundation of deep connections. Family travel fosters communication, teamwork, and mutual respect. It provides a platform for parents to be not just educators but also fellow explorers, sharing in the wonder and joy of discovery side by side with their children.

In an increasingly interconnected and rapidly changing world, the importance of travel and exploration for school-age children cannot be overstated. It ignites their curiosity, sparks their creativity, and nurtures their global awareness. Through travel, children become citizens of the world, armed with the knowledge, skills, and values necessary to thrive in an ever-evolving society. As we embark on this journey together, let us open the doors to the world, empowering our children to explore, learn, and grow in ways that no classroom can replicate.

Navigating the Adventure: Challenges and Considerations of Traveling with School-Age Children

Embarking on a journey with school-age children is like opening a treasure chest filled with joy, excitement, and endless possibilities. Traveling as a family creates unforgettable memories and strengthens bonds. However, let's face it—traveling with children brings its own set of challenges and considerations. From planning logistics to managing expectations, parents must navigate a path that ensures a smooth and enjoyable adventure for all. In this article, we delve into the realities of traveling with school-age children, offering insights and strategies to tackle the hurdles along the way.

Logistics and Planning:

When it comes to family travel, meticulous planning is key. Coordinating schedules, finding child-friendly accommodations, and mapping out itineraries can be daunting tasks. School-age children have their own routines, extracurricular activities, and educational commitments. Striking a balance between their academic needs and the travel itinerary is crucial. Planning ahead allows you to anticipate challenges, ensure a smooth transition, and maximize the educational opportunities presented by the destination.

Age-Appropriate Activities:

One of the primary considerations when traveling with school-age children is tailoring activities to their age group. While older children may enjoy historical tours, adventure sports, or immersive cultural experiences, younger children might prefer interactive museums, animal encounters, or nature walks. Striking a balance between activities that engage, educate, and entertain each child can be a juggling act. Researching age-appropriate activities beforehand ensures that the entire family can fully participate and enjoy the journey.

Keeping Them Engaged:

Children have boundless energy and short attention spans. The challenge lies in keeping them engaged throughout the trip. Long flights, train rides, or car journeys can test even the most patient parent. It is essential to pack entertainment options such as books, puzzles, and portable games to keep children occupied during transit. Additionally, involving them in the planning process, encouraging them to research the destination, and allowing them to have a say in the itinerary empowers them and keeps their interest levels high.

Safety and Security:

Traveling with school-age children means prioritizing their safety and security. As a parent, it's crucial to research the destination's safety measures, medical facilities, and emergency contact information. Taking precautions such as keeping a copy of important documents, setting clear rules and boundaries, and establishing a system to stay connected in crowded places can provide peace of mind. Educating children about personal safety, cultural norms, and respecting local customs adds an extra layer of security to the journey.

Flexibility and Patience:

Flexibility is the key to smooth family travel. Unexpected delays, weather changes, and unforeseen circumstances are part and parcel of any trip. Being prepared to adapt and adjust plans accordingly helps maintain a positive atmosphere. Patience is also vital when traveling with school-age children. They may have meltdowns, get tired easily, or express boredom. Understanding their needs, allowing downtime, and being patient during challenging moments creates a more harmonious travel experience for everyone.

Educational Opportunities:

Traveling with school-age children offers a unique opportunity to foster their education outside of the classroom. Every destination is a living textbook, teeming with history, culture, and natural wonders. Engaging children in educational activities, such as visiting museums, historical landmarks, or participating in local workshops, brings their learning to life. Encouraging them to journal their experiences, interview locals, or immerse themselves in the local language deepens their understanding and appreciation of the world around them.

Balancing Independence and Supervision:

As children grow older, they crave more independence. Balancing their desire for autonomy with the need for supervision can be challenging. Establishing guidelines based on their age, maturity, and destination helps strike a balance. Assigning them responsibilities, such as navigating or researching, empowers them and builds their confidence. However, it is essential to maintain vigilant supervision, especially in unfamiliar environments, to ensure their safety.

Traveling with school-age children is an adventure like no other, filled with laughter, discovery, and growth. While it comes with its own set of challenges and considerations, the rewards of exploring the world together as a family far outweigh the difficulties. By planning ahead, considering age-appropriate activities, prioritizing safety, nurturing their curiosity, and maintaining flexibility and patience, parents can create a memorable and transformative experience for their children. Embrace the challenges, adapt to the circumstances, and embark on a journey that will shape your family's bond and leave an indelible mark on your children's lives.

Embarking on an adventure with school-age children is an exhilarating experience that opens the doors to a world of wonder and discovery. As an experienced educator, a mother of three, and an avid traveler, I have witnessed firsthand the transformative power of travel for children. It is with immense pleasure and a deep passion for exploration that I present to you a travel guide tailored specifically for parents of school-age children.

This travel guide is more than just a collection of itineraries and tourist attractions. It is a comprehensive resource crafted with love and care, drawing upon my personal experiences as an educator, a parent, and an extensive traveler. Its purpose is to empower parents with the knowledge, insights, and practical strategies necessary to embark on a journey that not only enriches their children's lives but also strengthens family bonds.

Within the pages of this guide, you will find a wealth of valuable information and guidance, carefully curated to meet the unique needs and considerations of traveling with school-age children. From destination selection to logistics planning, from age-appropriate activities to safety and security measures, every aspect of family travel has been thoughtfully addressed.

I understand the challenges parents face when it comes to planning and executing a successful family trip. As an educator, I recognize the importance of aligning travel experiences with children's educational needs and interests. Hence, this guide is designed to infuse learning opportunities throughout the journey, transforming each destination into a vibrant classroom where children can broaden their horizons, ignite their curiosity, and deepen their understanding of the world.

Beyond practical tips and expert advice, this guide is infused with the heart and soul of a passionate traveler. I share personal anecdotes, relatable stories, and insights gained from years of traversing the globe with my own children. Through my experiences, I aim to inspire and encourage parents to embrace the joys and challenges of family travel, nurturing a sense of adventure and wonder within their children's hearts.

Whether you're planning a short weekend getaway or a long-haul international expedition, this travel guide will be your trusted companion, providing a roadmap for unforgettable experiences and meaningful connections. It will equip you with the tools to navigate the logistics, engage your children in age-appropriate activities, and create lifelong memories that will shape their growth and perspective.

Together, let's unlock the potential of travel and exploration for school-age children. Let's embark on a journey that transcends mere sightseeing, and instead, embraces the transformative power of experiencing the world with young, curious minds. Through this travel guide, let us weave a tapestry of unforgettable adventures, cherished moments, and a deep appreciation for the beauty and diversity of our planet.

Get ready to embark on an extraordinary journey with your school-age children. Adventure awaits, and this travel guide will be your trusted companion every step of the way. Let's create memories that will last a lifetime and nurture a love for exploration that will shape the lives of your children for years to come. Together, let's discover the world and make a lasting impact on the hearts and minds of our little travelers.

Chapter 2

Destination Selection - Exploring the World with Kids

The Johnson family embarked on a much-anticipated family vacation to a vibrant city known for its world-class museums. Eager to immerse themselves in art and history, they set their sights on a renowned museum filled with priceless masterpieces.

As they entered the grand museum, the children's eyes widened with excitement. Little Emma, the youngest of the clan, immediately noticed a sign that read, "No Touching the Exhibits." She grabbed her older brother, Alex, by the hand and whispered, "Alex, don't touch anything!"

The family began their museum exploration, marveling at ancient artifacts and famous paintings. They moved from room to room, soaking in the cultural treasures around them. However, as they entered the room housing a delicate sculpture, chaos ensued.

Emma's curiosity got the best of her, and she couldn't resist getting closer to the sculpture. She leaned forward, her little finger extending towards the artwork. But in a moment of misjudgment, her hand brushed against the sculpture, causing it to wobble precariously.

Time seemed to slow down as the sculpture teetered on the edge of disaster. The Johnson family froze, their eyes wide with horror, as the sculpture crashed to the ground, shattered into pieces.

The silence that followed was deafening, and the family found themselves surrounded by stunned museum visitors and security guards. Emma's eyes filled with tears as she realized the magnitude of her innocent mistake.

The museum staff rushed over, trying to assess the situation while suppressing their shock. Meanwhile, Alex, always the quick thinker, stepped forward and took responsibility, exclaiming, "I couldn't resist giving the artwork a high-five! It's just so impressive!"

The security guards looked at each other, trying to stifle their laughter, before escorting the family to a nearby office to sort out the incident. In that moment, the tension broke, and the entire family burst into laughter, realizing the absurdity of the situation.

The museum staff, amused by Alex's creative explanation, quickly understood that it was an unintentional mishap. They even shared stories of other peculiar incidents involving their precious exhibits.

After a thorough apology and a promise to contribute to the repair costs, the Johnsons were released from the office with a newfound bond with the museum staff. As they continued exploring, their adventure became a running joke throughout the museum, with other visitors giving them playful nods and smiles.

The Johnson family walked away from the museum that day, not only with memories of beautiful artwork but also with a hilarious family tale to be passed down for generations. And while they may not be invited back to that particular museum anytime soon, they had learned a valuable lesson about the importance of looking but not touching, and the enduring power of laughter even in the face of unexpected accidents.

Embarking on a family travel adventure is an exciting prospect, filled with the promise of new experiences, unforgettable memories, and quality time spent together. However, one crucial element often overlooked by parents is the careful selection of the destination.

Choosing the right destination for your family can make all the difference in ensuring a smooth, enjoyable, and enriching journey for everyone involved. In this article, we will explore the profound importance of destination selection for family travel and how it can unlock adventures and create lasting memories.

Tailoring to Family-Friendly Environments:

When planning a trip with kids, it's essential to choose destinations that offer family-friendly environments. These are places designed to cater to the needs and interests of children, ensuring a comfortable and engaging experience for the whole family. Family-friendly destinations often provide a range of amenities, including kid-friendly accommodations, restaurants with children's menus, safe playgrounds, and attractions specifically tailored for young visitors. By selecting such destinations, parents can enjoy peace of mind, knowing that their children's needs are prioritized.

Age-Appropriate Activities:

Every child is unique, with varying interests, preferences, and developmental stages. Destination selection allows parents to align their travel plans with age-appropriate activities and attractions. For instance, young children might enjoy interactive museums, animal encounters, or theme parks, while older kids might be more interested in historical sites, outdoor adventures, or cultural experiences. Choosing destinations that offer a diverse range of activities ensures that each family member can find something to suit their interests, fostering enthusiasm, and a sense of engagement throughout the journey.

Safety and Security:

The safety and security of our loved ones are paramount, especially when traveling to unfamiliar places. Destination selection plays a critical role in ensuring a secure environment for family travel. By conducting thorough research and considering factors such as crime rates, political stability, and healthcare facilities, parents can make informed decisions about where to take their children. Opting for destinations with a reputation for safety helps alleviate concerns and allows families to focus on creating positive and worry-free memories.

Educational Opportunities:

Family travel presents a unique opportunity for children to expand their horizons and learn about the world beyond their textbooks. Selecting destinations that offer rich educational opportunities allows families to combine fun and learning seamlessly. Historical sites, museums, cultural festivals, and interactive exhibits can ignite children's curiosity, spark their imagination, and deepen their understanding of different cultures, history, and the natural world. By choosing educational destinations, parents can provide their children with hands-on experiences that foster personal growth and a lifelong love of learning.

Building Bonds and Shared Experiences:

Family travel is more than just visiting attractions; it's about strengthening bonds and creating shared experiences. Destination selection plays a crucial role in facilitating this process. When choosing a destination, consider activities that encourage interaction and quality time together, such as hiking through breathtaking landscapes, exploring local markets, trying new cuisines, or embarking on adventure sports as a family. These shared adventures provide opportunities for parents and children to connect, communicate, and create lifelong memories that will be cherished for years to come.

Cultural Sensitivity and Global Understanding:

In an increasingly interconnected world, exposing children to different cultures, traditions, and perspectives is vital. By carefully selecting destinations that offer diverse cultural experiences, parents can help foster cultural sensitivity and global understanding in their children. Exploring local customs, traditions, and languages enables kids to develop empathy, respect for diversity, and a broader worldview. These experiences lay the foundation for raising well-rounded individuals who appreciate and respect different cultures throughout their lives.

The importance of destination selection for family travel cannot be overstated. It sets the stage for a successful, enriching, and memorable journey for parents and children alike. From tailoring to family-friendly environments and age-appropriate activities to ensuring safety, unlocking educational opportunities, and fostering bonds through shared experiences, choosing the right destination is the key to unlocking the full potential of family travel. So, take the time to research, plan, and select destinations that cater to your family's unique interests and needs. Embrace the power of destination selection, and embark on a journey of exploration, adventure, and unforgettable memories with your loved ones.

Unlocking the Perfect Journey: The Importance of Researching and Identifying Suitable Destinations When Traveling with Kids

Planning a trip with kids requires careful consideration and thorough research to ensure a smooth and enjoyable experience for the whole family. From finding family-friendly accommodations to identifying age-appropriate activities and ensuring safety, researching and identifying suitable destinations play a pivotal role in creating a memorable and stress-free journey. In this article, we will explore the importance of researching and identifying suitable destinations when traveling with kids and how it sets the foundation for an unforgettable adventure.

Tailoring to Family-Friendly Environments:

Researching and identifying family-friendly destinations enable parents to find environments that are specifically designed to cater to the needs and interests of children. These destinations offer a range of amenities, including accommodations with family-friendly facilities, restaurants with kid-friendly menus, and attractions suitable for young visitors. By selecting such destinations, parents can ensure a comfortable and welcoming environment where their children can thrive, allowing the whole family to relax and enjoy the vacation.

Age-Appropriate Activities and Attractions:

Every child has different interests and preferences, which evolve as they grow. Researching and identifying suitable destinations allows parents to align their travel plans with age-appropriate activities and attractions. For younger children, destinations with interactive museums, zoos, and theme parks might be ideal. Older kids may enjoy historical sites, adventure sports, or cultural experiences. By choosing destinations that offer a diverse range of activities, parents can ensure that each family member finds something to engage and excite them throughout the trip.

Safety and Security:

The safety and security of children are paramount when traveling as a family. Thorough research helps parents identify destinations with a reputation for safety, including low crime rates, stable political situations, and reliable healthcare facilities. It is crucial to consider factors such as travel advisories, local laws and customs, and the availability of emergency services. By choosing destinations with a strong emphasis on safety, parents can enjoy peace of mind, allowing them to focus on creating lasting memories with their children.

Accessibility and Convenience:

Traveling with kids often involves logistical considerations, such as transportation, accessibility, and convenience. Researching and identifying suitable destinations enable parents to plan for the smoothest travel experience possible. Considerations such as flight connections, proximity to airports, availability of public transportation, and the ease of navigating the destination with strollers or wheelchairs should be taken into account. By selecting destinations that offer convenient transportation options and accessible infrastructure, parents can minimize stress and maximize enjoyment during the journey.

Budget-Friendly Options:

Family travel comes with financial considerations, and researching destinations allows parents to find budget-friendly options without compromising on the overall experience. By exploring different destinations, comparing prices of accommodations, activities, and dining options, parents can create a realistic budget and make informed decisions about where to spend their money. Researching the availability of discounts, family packages, and free attractions in the destination can further optimize the travel budget, allowing families to maximize their experiences within their means.

Cultural Sensitivity and Learning Opportunities:

Family travel presents a unique opportunity to expose children to different cultures and foster global understanding. Researching destinations helps parents identify places that offer rich cultural experiences, enabling children to learn about traditions, customs, and local history. This exposure enhances their cultural sensitivity, broadens their perspectives, and fosters empathy and respect for diversity. By selecting destinations that provide learning opportunities, parents can create an educational and immersive experience that enriches their children's understanding of the world.

Researching and identifying suitable destinations is an essential step in planning a successful family trip. It allows parents to tailor their travel plans to the specific needs and interests of their children, ensuring a family-friendly environment, age-appropriate activities, safety, accessibility, and budget-friendly options. By investing time in research, parents can unlock the perfect journey that offers enriching experiences, creates lasting memories, and strengthens family bonds. So, embrace the importance of researching and identifying suitable destinations, and embark on a remarkable adventure that delights, educates, and brings joy to your entire family.

Exploring the World Together: Popular Family Travel Destinations Worldwide

When it comes to family travel, the world is your playground. There are countless destinations around the globe that cater to the needs and interests of families, offering a wide array of attractions and activities for all ages. From thrilling theme parks to breathtaking natural wonders and culturally rich cities, popular family travel destinations provide opportunities for bonding, adventure, and creating lifelong memories. In this article, we will embark on a journey to explore some of the most popular family travel destinations worldwide, inspiring you to plan your next unforgettable family adventure.

Orlando, Florida, USA:

Orlando, often referred to as the "Theme Park Capital of the World," is a dream destination for families seeking exhilarating adventures. Home to Walt Disney World Resort, Universal Orlando Resort, and SeaWorld Orlando, the city offers endless entertainment options for children of all ages. From meeting beloved characters to riding thrilling roller coasters and exploring immersive worlds, Orlando is a magical place where dreams come true for both kids and adults alike.

Tokyo, Japan:

Tokyo is a vibrant metropolis that seamlessly blends tradition and innovation, making it an exciting destination for families. The city boasts an array of family-friendly attractions, including Tokyo Disneyland and DisneySea, where kids can immerse themselves in the magic of Disney. In addition, Tokyo offers interactive museums, such as the National Museum of Nature and Science and the Tokyo Science Museum, where children can explore the wonders of science and technology through hands-on exhibits.

Sydney, Australia:

Sydney, with its iconic landmarks and stunning natural beauty, is a fantastic family destination. The city's most famous attraction, the Sydney Opera House, offers guided tours suitable for children, allowing them to discover the world of performing arts. Families can also enjoy a visit to Taronga Zoo, where kids can get up close and personal with native Australian animals. Bondi Beach provides a perfect setting for sun, sand, and surf, while the Royal Botanic Garden offers a peaceful retreat amidst the bustling city.

London, United Kingdom:

London is a treasure trove of family-friendly experiences, blending history, culture, and entertainment. The British Museum showcases fascinating artifacts from around the world, while the Natural History Museum captivates young minds with its dinosaur exhibits. Families can enjoy a walk through Hyde Park or a boat ride along the River Thames, taking in the city's iconic sights. Not to be missed is a visit to Warner Bros. Studio Tour London - The Making of Harry Potter, where fans of the beloved series can step into the magical world of Hogwarts.

Cape Town, South Africa:

Cape Town offers a unique blend of natural beauty and cultural experiences, making it an excellent destination for families seeking adventure and diversity. The city is surrounded by stunning landscapes, including Table Mountain and the Cape Peninsula, where families can hike, take cable car rides, or embark on thrilling wildlife safaris. Kids can learn about marine life at the Two Oceans Aquarium or explore the interactive exhibits at the Cape Town Science Centre. Cape Town also provides opportunities for educational experiences, such as visiting the historic Robben Island, where Nelson Mandela was once imprisoned.

Bali, Indonesia:

Bali is an idyllic paradise that offers a wealth of experiences for families. The island's pristine beaches provide opportunities for relaxation and water activities, while its lush landscapes offer breathtaking scenery to explore. Families can visit the sacred Monkey Forest in Ubud, interact with gentle giants at the Elephant Safari Park, or embark on a cultural journey through traditional Balinese dance performances and temple visits. Bali's warm hospitality and kid-friendly resorts make it a haven for families seeking both adventure and relaxation.

The world is filled with popular family travel destinations that promise adventure, learning, and unforgettable experiences. Whether you're seeking the magic of theme parks, the awe-inspiring wonders of nature, or the cultural richness of iconic cities, there is a destination to suit every family's preferences and interests. From the enchantment of Orlando and Tokyo to the cultural treasures of London and Cape Town, and the tropical paradise of Bali, these destinations invite families to come together, explore, and create lifelong memories. So, pack your bags, embark on an extraordinary family adventure, and discover the wonders that await in these popular family travel destinations worldwide.

Chapter 3

Planning and Preparation - Laying the Foundation for a Memorable Trip

The Smith family embarked on a sunny adventure to the beautiful Florida Keys. With their suitcases packed and excitement in the air, they were ready for a vacation filled with laughter, relaxation, and unforgettable memories.

Their first day began with a visit to a pristine beach with crystal-clear waters. As they set up their spot in the sand, little Emily's eyes widened in awe. She couldn't wait to dive into the inviting ocean waves.

But as she ran towards the water, a sneaky seagull swooped down, snatching her sandwich right out of her hand. Emily stood frozen, her mouth hanging open in disbelief, while the seagull flew away triumphantly with its stolen prize.

The entire family burst into laughter, watching the seagull enjoy its impromptu beach picnic. Emily, although initially shocked, couldn't help but find the humor in the situation. She declared herself the "Seagull Food Olympics Champion" and vowed to be more vigilant with her snacks from that point forward.

The next day, the Smiths embarked on a snorkeling adventure. As they explored the vibrant coral reefs and swam alongside colorful fish, they were greeted by a surprise visitor—a friendly dolphin.

The dolphin, seemingly drawn to the kids' laughter and splashing, swam playfully around them. It performed flips, twirls, and even gave them a friendly nudge, as if inviting them to join in the aquatic fun.

The Smith family was overjoyed, their faces beaming with delight. The kids took turns trying to mimic the dolphin's acrobatic moves, flapping their arms and doing their best dolphin impressions. They laughed and splashed, creating a joyful symphony of laughter that echoed throughout the ocean.

The encounter with the dolphin became the highlight of their trip, and they left the snorkeling spot with hearts full of gratitude for the magical connection they had experienced with nature.

As the sun began to set on their last day in the Florida Keys, the Smiths gathered on a tranquil beach, ready to witness a breathtaking sunset. They held hands, their toes sinking into the warm sand, and exchanged stories of their adventures and the laughter that had filled their days.

As the vibrant hues painted the sky, little Jacob turned to his parents and said, "This is the best vacation ever! Can we do it again next year?" The family shared a collective smile, realizing that this trip had brought them closer together, created cherished memories, and sparked a lifelong love for exploring the world as a family.

And so, with hearts full of gratitude and a renewed sense of adventure, the Smiths bid farewell to the Florida Keys, knowing that the beauty of their time spent there would forever be etched in their hearts.

Picture this: you're on a beautiful sandy beach, the sun gently warming your skin, and a refreshing ocean breeze caressing your face. But wait, you're not alone—your school-age kids are by your side, their eyes wide with wonder as they explore the vibrant marine life just beyond the shoreline. Laughter fills the air as you build sandcastles together, creating memories that will last a lifetime.

Traveling with school-age kids can be an incredibly rewarding experience, but it also requires careful planning and preparation. The secret to a successful trip lies in laying a solid foundation, setting the stage for a truly memorable adventure that caters to the unique needs and interests of your children.

Why is planning and preparation so crucial when embarking on a family journey? Well, let's imagine for a moment what it would be like to arrive at your destination unprepared. The stress of finding suitable activities for your children, the frustration of discovering that your accommodation isn't child-friendly, and the disappointment of missed opportunities—all these can turn your dream vacation into a nightmare.

By taking the time to plan and prepare, you can anticipate the needs of your school-age kids and ensure a smooth and enjoyable trip for the entire family. It's not just about finding the perfect destination or booking the right flights; it's about creating a balance between educational experiences and recreational fun, fostering family bonding, and weaving together the threads of an unforgettable adventure.

Throughout this chapter, we will delve into the essential aspects of planning and preparation when traveling with school-age kids. From assessing your needs and selecting the perfect destination to making necessary health and safety preparations, and packing smartly, we'll cover it all.

But remember, the key to success lies in setting realistic expectations. Traveling with children brings its own set of challenges, but with proper planning, these challenges can transform into opportunities for growth and discovery. So, let's dive in and lay the foundation for a trip that will be etched in your family's memories for years to come. Together, we'll unlock the secrets to crafting an extraordinary adventure that caters to the needs and dreams of your school-age kids.

Anticipating and Addressing the Unique Needs of School-Age Children: A Guide to Traveling in the US and Abroad

Traveling with school-age children can be an incredible opportunity to broaden their horizons, expose them to new cultures, and create lifelong memories. Whether you're exploring the diverse landscapes of the United States or venturing abroad to immerse yourselves in unfamiliar territories, it's important to anticipate and address the unique needs of your children to ensure a smooth and enjoyable journey. In this article, we'll delve into some essential considerations for traveling with school-age kids, both within the United States and abroad.

Educational Engagement:

One of the advantages of traveling with school-age children is the opportunity to enhance their education beyond the classroom. When planning your trip, consider destinations that offer educational experiences and activities. For example, in the United States, you can explore historical sites like the Freedom Trail in Boston, the Smithsonian museums in Washington, D.C., or the Space Center in Houston. Abroad, you can visit ancient ruins, art galleries, or cultural landmarks that bring history and geography to life. Engaging your children in educational activities will not only foster their curiosity and love for learning but also make the journey more enriching for the whole family.

Safety and Security:

The safety and security of your children should be a top priority when traveling, regardless of your destination. Within the United States, familiarize yourself with the local safety guidelines, emergency contact numbers, and any potential risks in the area you plan to visit. Abroad, research the safety standards, political stability, and any travel advisories issued by your home country. It's also important to teach your children about personal safety measures, such as staying close to you in crowded places, not talking to strangers, and being aware of their surroundings. By addressing safety concerns proactively, you can ensure peace of mind throughout your journey.

Cultural Sensitivity:

Traveling provides an excellent opportunity for children to learn about different cultures, customs, and traditions. Encourage your school-age kids to embrace diversity and respect the local culture wherever you go. Before your trip, educate them about the basic etiquette and customs of the destination. For example, in the United States, they can learn about the cultural significance of Native American traditions or the diverse customs of different states. When traveling abroad, teach them common phrases and greetings in the local language, and discuss cultural norms such as appropriate dress and behavior. By fostering cultural sensitivity, you'll not only enhance your children's global awareness but also create positive interactions with locals.

Health and Well-being:

Maintaining your children's health and well-being during your travels is essential. Within the United States, ensure that your children are up to date with their vaccinations and carry any necessary medical records or prescriptions. If you're traveling abroad, research the specific health requirements for the destination, such as vaccinations, malaria prophylaxis, or food and water safety precautions. It's also wise to pack a comprehensive first aid kit with essential supplies for any minor injuries or illnesses. Additionally, encourage your children to practice good hygiene habits, such as frequent handwashing and using sunscreen, to keep them healthy and protected throughout the journey.

Entertainment and Recreation:

While educational experiences are valuable, it's equally important to provide opportunities for relaxation, fun, and recreation during your travels. Research family-friendly activities and attractions in your chosen destination. In the United States, you can visit theme parks, national parks, or enjoy outdoor adventures like hiking or camping. When traveling abroad, seek out child-friendly museums, amusement parks, or family-oriented tours and excursions. Consider your children's interests and hobbies when planning activities, allowing them to engage in age-appropriate entertainment that caters to their preferences. Balancing educational experiences with recreational activities will ensure a well-rounded and enjoyable trip for everyone involved.

Communication and Engagement:

Traveling with school-age children can be a great bonding experience, and it's important to foster communication and engagement throughout the journey. Encourage your children to actively participate in the planning process, allowing them to voice their opinions and contribute to decision-making. During the trip, involve them in age-appropriate activities, such as map reading, photography, or journaling, to keep them engaged and excited. Encourage open dialogue, where they can share their thoughts, observations, and questions about the places they visit. By nurturing communication and engagement, you'll create lasting memories and strengthen family bonds.

In conclusion, traveling with school-age children offers an incredible opportunity for exploration, education, and family bonding. Whether you're traversing the diverse landscapes of the United States or immersing yourselves in the rich tapestry of international destinations, anticipating and addressing the unique needs of your children is crucial. By considering educational engagement, safety and security, cultural sensitivity, health and well-being, entertainment and recreation, and fostering communication and engagement, you'll lay the groundwork for a rewarding and memorable travel experience. So, pack your bags, embark on this adventure together, and watch as your school-age children's horizons expand, their curiosity grows, and their love for travel blossoms.

Balancing Fun and Educational Activities:
Tips and Tricks for Traveling with School-Age Children

As a parent, you want your children to have a blast while traveling, but you also understand the importance of educational experiences. The good news is that you don't have to choose between fun and learning when planning your family adventures. With a bit of thoughtful planning and creativity, you can strike the perfect balance between entertaining activities and educational opportunities. In this article, we'll explore some tips and tricks to help you create an unforgettable trip that combines both fun and learning for your school-age children.

Research Ahead of Time:

Before embarking on your journey, spend some time researching your destination. Look for attractions, museums, historical sites, or cultural experiences that offer educational value. Find interactive exhibits, guided tours, or workshops specifically designed for children. Make a list of these activities and choose a few that align with your children's interests and the overall theme of your trip. By planning ahead, you'll ensure that you don't miss out on the educational gems your destination has to offer.

Mix and Match:

When planning your daily itinerary, aim for a mix of fun and educational activities. Alternate between visits to museums, historical sites, or science centers with recreational activities like visiting theme parks, playgrounds, or engaging in outdoor adventures. This way, your children can absorb knowledge while having fun and staying engaged throughout the trip. Mixing and matching activities will keep their interest levels high and prevent boredom.

Transform Sightseeing into a Game:

Transforming sightseeing into a game can be a fun and interactive way to engage your children while exploring a new place. Create scavenger hunts or treasure hunts where they have to find specific landmarks, artifacts, or pieces of information. Provide them with a list of questions or tasks related to the sights they will encounter. For example, they can interview locals, take photos of specific landmarks, or collect brochures to learn more about the history or culture of the area. By turning sightseeing into a game, you'll encourage active participation and ensure a memorable learning experience.

Use Technology Wisely:

Harness the power of technology to enhance your children's learning experiences while on the road. Before your trip, download educational apps, interactive maps, or language learning tools that can be used offline. These resources can provide valuable information, quizzes, and interactive content about the places you visit. Additionally, encourage your children to document their travel experiences through photography or journaling using digital devices. This not only enhances their creativity but also allows them to reflect on their experiences and develop their communication skills.

Engage Local Guides or Tours:

When exploring a new destination, consider engaging local guides or joining guided tours. Local guides can offer insights into the history, culture, and traditions of the place, making the learning experience more immersive and engaging for your children. Look for family-oriented tours that cater specifically to school-age kids. These tours often involve hands-on activities, storytelling, or interactive demonstrations that bring the destination to life. Local guides can provide a deeper understanding of the local culture, allowing your children to connect with the place on a more meaningful level.

Embrace Experiential Learning:

Sometimes the most powerful learning experiences come from immersing oneself in a new environment. Encourage your children to interact with locals, try traditional foods, or participate in cultural activities. Visiting local markets, attending festivals or workshops, or engaging in community service projects are excellent ways to expose your children to different perspectives and broaden their understanding of the world. Experiential learning not only fosters a sense of cultural appreciation but also encourages empathy and global citizenship.

Incorporate Learning into Everyday Moments:

Remember that learning can happen even in the most ordinary moments of your journey. Whether you're waiting in line, traveling on public transportation, or enjoying a meal together, seize these opportunities to spark conversations and encourage curiosity. Discuss the local language, customs, or geography. Encourage your children to ask questions and observe their surroundings. By incorporating learning into everyday moments, you'll make the trip a continuous educational experience.

Reflect and Share:

After each day of exploration, take some time to reflect and share your experiences as a family. Encourage your children to express their thoughts, feelings, and newfound knowledge. This can be done through group discussions, art projects, or even creating a travel journal. Reflecting and sharing not only solidifies the educational aspects of the trip but also strengthens family bonds and creates lasting memories.

In conclusion, balancing fun and educational activities is not only possible but also highly rewarding when traveling with school-age children. By researching ahead of time, mixing and matching activities, turning sightseeing into a game, utilizing technology wisely, engaging local guides, embracing experiential learning, incorporating learning into everyday moments, and reflecting and sharing as a family, you can create an unforgettable journey that combines fun, adventure, and valuable educational experiences. So go ahead and plan your next family trip with confidence, knowing that you are fostering a love for learning and creating lifelong memories for your school-age children.

Involving Children in the Planning Process: Empowering Young Travelers for an Unforgettable Journey

When it comes to family travel, involving children in the planning process can transform a trip from a mere vacation into an enriching and empowering adventure. By giving your children a voice in the decision-making and allowing them to actively contribute to the travel plans, you not only ignite their excitement and curiosity but also instill a sense of ownership and responsibility. In this article, we'll explore some tips and tricks to involve children in the planning process, ensuring that their interests and preferences are considered, and setting the stage for an unforgettable journey together.

Start with Destination Exploration:

Begin by exploring different destinations together as a family. Provide your children with options that align with your travel goals, budget, and time constraints. Use travel guides, books, websites, and even documentaries to introduce them to the various possibilities. Encourage them to research and present their findings on different locations, highlighting the unique attractions and activities that appeal to them. By involving them in the initial stage of destination exploration, you foster their engagement and curiosity right from the start.

Encourage Wish Lists:

Ask your children to create wish lists of activities, landmarks, or experiences they would love to have during the trip. These can range from visiting a specific museum or theme park to trying out local cuisine or engaging in outdoor adventures. Encourage them to brainstorm and think outside the box. This will not only give you insights into their interests but also provide an opportunity for discussion and compromise as a family. Consider incorporating some of their ideas into the final travel itinerary to make it more personalized and exciting for everyone.

Involve Children in Research:

Once the destination is chosen, involve your children in the research process. Assign them age-appropriate tasks, such as finding information about the history, culture, or famous landmarks of the chosen location. They can browse the internet, read books, or interview people who have visited the place before. Encourage them to gather interesting facts, create a scrapbook, or even give short presentations to share their findings. This research phase not only educates them about the destination but also encourages their engagement and active participation in the planning process.

Collaborate on Itinerary Planning:

Sit down together as a family and collaboratively plan the travel itinerary. Share the responsibility of creating a day-to-day schedule that incorporates both fun and educational activities. Discuss the possibilities, weigh the pros and cons of different options, and make decisions as a team. Encourage your children to voice their opinions and preferences, and be open to compromising when necessary. By involving them in the itinerary planning, you not only ensure that their interests are considered but also foster a sense of ownership and excitement for the upcoming journey.

Budgeting and Financial Education:

Integrate financial education into the planning process by involving your children in budgeting discussions. Explain the concept of budgeting and the importance of making choices based on available resources. Assign them tasks such as researching accommodation options, transportation costs, or entrance fees for attractions. Encourage them to compare prices, look for deals or discounts, and contribute ideas for saving money. This exercise not only helps them understand the value of money but also instills responsible financial habits from a young age.

Packing and Essential Item Checklist:

Engage your children in the packing process by creating a checklist of essential items together. Discuss the climate and activities of the destination to help them choose appropriate clothing, footwear, and accessories. Encourage them to pack their own essentials, allowing them to take responsibility for their belongings. This not only teaches them organization and independence but also ensures they have the items they need for a comfortable journey. Additionally, consider involving them in creating an entertainment pack with books, games, or travel-friendly activities to keep them engaged during the trip.

Documenting the Journey:

Encourage your children to document the journey through photographs, videos, or journaling. Provide them with cameras or smartphones (with appropriate supervision) to capture their unique perspectives and experiences. Encourage them to write about their favorite moments, interesting facts, or even create a scrapbook or a digital travel journal. This not only allows them to express their creativity but also serves as a precious memento of their travel adventures. Sharing their documentation with family and friends after the trip can be a source of pride and accomplishment.

Reflection and Post-Trip Sharing:

After the trip, take the time to reflect and share your experiences as a family. Encourage your children to discuss their favorite memories, the things they learned, and how the trip has impacted them. Create opportunities for them to present their experiences through photos, stories, or even a small presentation. This reflection process not only reinforces the educational aspects of travel but also strengthens family bonds and provides closure to the journey.

Involving children in the planning process not only empowers them but also creates a sense of anticipation and excitement for the upcoming adventure. By starting with destination exploration, encouraging wish lists, involving them in research, collaborating on itinerary planning, integrating financial education, engaging them in packing, documenting the journey, and reflecting on the experience afterward, you'll create a memorable trip that caters to their interests and fosters a love for travel and exploration. So, embark on your next family adventure together, knowing that you have empowered your young travelers to become active participants in the planning process.

Chapter 4

Pack Like a Pro - Gear Up for an Exciting Journey

The Suarez family embarked on a thrilling trip to the vibrant city of Toronto, Canada. As they arrived, their excitement reached new heights, fueled by the anticipation of exploring a new country together.

Their first stop was the famous CN Tower, a towering structure that offered breathtaking views of the city. The kids, Carlos and Sofia, were in awe of the impressive height and couldn't wait to reach the observation deck.

As the family stepped into the glass elevator, ready for a thrilling ascent, Carlos suddenly realized he had left his favorite baseball cap in the car. Desperate not to miss out on the experience, he made a split-second decision and darted out of the elevator just as the doors closed.

The rest of the family watched in shock as the elevator began to ascend, leaving Carlos stranded on the ground floor. He frantically waved his arms, hoping to catch their attention, but his efforts were in vain.

Meanwhile, the elevator continued its ascent, and as the family reached the observation deck, they were met with stunning panoramic views of the city. However, their joy was quickly replaced with concern for Carlos.

Back on the ground floor, Carlos realized he had to find a way to reunite with his family. Determined not to miss out on the experience, he spotted a staircase and sprinted up, flight after flight, taking the stairs while his family soared above him in the elevator.

As Carlos reached the top of the stairs, panting and out of breath, he stumbled onto the observation deck, startling his family and nearby visitors. Sofia burst into laughter, unable to contain her amusement at Carlos' unexpected solo adventure.

The Suarez family, now reunited, joined in on the laughter, realizing that Carlos had unwittingly created a memorable tale to be shared for years to come. They took a family photo, with Carlos proudly wearing his baseball cap, signaling the triumphant completion of his stair-climbing feat.

Throughout the rest of their trip, the Suarez family lovingly teased Carlos about his "elevator chase" and turned it into a running joke. Every time they entered an elevator, they would jokingly ask Carlos if he was sure he had everything he needed.

The laughter and camaraderie they shared during their time in Toronto became the true highlight of their trip. The Suarez family returned home with not only fond memories of a beautiful city but also a priceless anecdote that would bring them joy and laughter for years to come.

Get ready to embark on an unforgettable adventure with your school-age kids! As you prepare for your upcoming trip, it's crucial to ensure that you have all the essential gear to make your journey smooth, comfortable, and enjoyable for everyone. From practical packing tips to exciting entertainment options, this chapter will guide you through the must-have gear for a seamless travel experience. Let's dive in and discover how to pack like a pro!

Travel Essentials for School Age Kids:

Packing checklist for school-age children:
Before setting off on your journey, it's essential to have a comprehensive packing checklist tailored specifically to your school-age kids. Take into account the duration of your trip, the climate of your destination, and any special activities you have planned. Don't forget to pack their favorite clothes, pajamas, and extra layers for unexpected weather changes. Ensure you have enough underwear and socks to last the entire trip, and don't overlook essentials like hats, gloves, and scarves for cooler destinations.

Suitable luggage options for kids:
Choosing the right luggage for your little travelers is key to their comfort and independence. Opt for lightweight suitcases or rolling duffel bags that they can easily manage themselves. Consider picking luggage with vibrant colors or fun patterns to add an element of excitement to their travel experience. Additionally, packing cubes or organizers can help keep their belongings neat and easily accessible throughout the trip.

Travel-friendly backpacks and daypacks:

Encourage your school-age kids to have their own backpack or daypack, filled with items they'll need during the journey. These can include their favorite toys, books, and snacks to keep them engaged and entertained while on the move. Look for backpacks with comfortable padding and adjustable straps to ensure a proper fit. Bonus tip: Personalize their backpacks with patches or pins representing their interests, making them feel extra special and ready for adventure!

Comfortable and supportive shoes for active adventures:
When it comes to exploring new destinations, comfortable and supportive footwear is essential for school-age kids. Opt for sneakers or closed-toe shoes that provide adequate arch support and cushioning. If you plan on engaging in outdoor activities or hiking, consider packing a pair of sturdy and waterproof shoes. Let your kids participate in

choosing their footwear, and they'll be excited to put their best foot forward on the journey ahead!

Weather-appropriate clothing and accessories:

Being prepared for various weather conditions ensures that your kids stay comfortable and enjoy every moment of your trip. Pack lightweight and breathable clothing for warmer climates, including t-shirts, shorts, and swimsuits. For cooler destinations, pack layers like sweaters, jackets, and pants. Don't forget to include essential accessories like sunglasses, hats, and umbrellas to protect your little ones from the sun or rain.

Personal hygiene and toiletry items:

Maintaining personal hygiene routines is crucial, even while traveling. Pack travel-sized toiletries such as toothbrushes, toothpaste, shampoo, and soap. Include any necessary medications your children might need, along with a small first aid kit for minor emergencies. Hand sanitizer, wet wipes, and tissues are also handy for on-the-go cleanliness. With these essentials in tow, you'll be prepared for any travel-related hygiene needs that may arise.

Entertainment and Technology on the Go:

Portable entertainment options for long journeys:
Long journeys can be tiring, but keeping your school-age kids entertained will make the time fly by. Pack a variety of portable entertainment options, such as handheld gaming devices, tablets, or portable DVD players loaded with their favorite movies or TV shows. Engage their imagination with activity books, sticker sets, or travel-themed coloring books. Surprise them with new and exciting toys or puzzles to unveil during the journey. The possibilities are endless!

Electronics and gadgets suitable for kids:
In the digital age, electronics play a significant role in keeping kids engaged during travel. Ensure you have chargers and adapters for all the electronic devices you plan to bring along. Consider child-friendly headphones to keep the noise level down and provide a more immersive experience for your kids. You can also download educational apps or audiobooks to make the journey both entertaining and informative.

Travel-friendly board games and card games:

Unplug and enjoy some quality time together as a family with travel-friendly board games and card games. Look for compact versions of popular games like UNO, Connect Four, or travel-sized magnetic chess sets. These games are not only entertaining but also promote bonding and friendly competition among family members. The best part? They can be enjoyed during long layovers, train rides, or even cozy evenings at your accommodation.

Books, magazines, and coloring supplies:

Encourage your kids to dive into the world of reading during your travels. Allow them to select a few of their favorite books or magazines to bring along, keeping their minds engaged and sparking their imagination. Coloring supplies like colored pencils or washable markers, along with travel-sized sketchbooks, are also fantastic options to unleash their creativity during downtime or while waiting for transportation.

Headphones and earbuds for personal entertainment:

To provide your school-age kids with personal entertainment options, don't forget to pack headphones or earbuds. These allow them to enjoy their favorite music, podcasts, or audio stories without disturbing fellow travelers. Make sure the headphones are comfortable, adjustable, and suitable for children to avoid discomfort during prolonged use. With their favorite tunes in their ears, your kids will be immersed in their own world of adventure.

By equipping yourself with the right gear and entertainment options, you'll set the stage for an extraordinary journey with your school-age kids. From carefully selecting comfortable clothing and travel-friendly luggage to packing exciting entertainment options, this chapter has covered all the essentials for a smooth and enjoyable trip. With these must-have gear items in tow, get ready to embark on an adventure filled with precious memories and endless fun for the whole family!

Safety First - Protecting and Nurturing your Adventurous Explorers!

As you embark on an exciting journey with your school-age kids, their safety and well-being are of utmost importance. This chapter is dedicated to providing you with the essential knowledge and practical tips to ensure a secure and healthy travel experience for your little adventurers. From health essentials and precautions to childproofing your travel environment, let's dive into a world of colorful information and engage in the art of worry-free travel!

Health Essentials for School Age Travelers:

Required vaccinations and medical preparations:
Before jetting off to your dream destination, it's vital to prioritize your children's health. Research the required vaccinations for your travel destination well in advance and ensure your kids are up to date with their immunizations. Consult with your healthcare provider for any additional precautions or medications that might be necessary based on your specific travel plans. By taking these proactive steps, you're not only safeguarding your children but also promoting a healthy journey.

Prescription medications and first aid supplies:

When traveling with school-age kids, it's essential to pack all necessary prescription medications they require. Make sure to carry an ample supply for the duration of your trip, along with a copy of the prescriptions. Additionally, assemble a comprehensive first aid kit tailored to the needs of your children, including bandages, antiseptics, pain relievers, and any specific medications for common ailments they might experience. This way, you'll be well-prepared to handle minor health issues that may arise during your travels.

Travel insurance and emergency contact information:
No adventure is complete without a safety net. Acquire comprehensive travel insurance that covers any potential medical emergencies and travel-related mishaps. Familiarize yourself with the policy details, including emergency medical services, evacuation coverage, and 24/7 assistance. It's also crucial to carry a list of emergency contact numbers for your home country and the local authorities at your destination. Having this information readily available will give you peace of mind and ensure quick and efficient support in case of an emergency.

Tips for dealing with common travel-related health issues:
During your travels, it's not uncommon for children to experience minor health issues such as motion sickness, allergies, or stomach upsets. Prepare yourself by researching remedies and preventative measures for these common ailments. For example, motion sickness bands or medications can alleviate discomfort during long car rides or boat trips. By being proactive and well-informed, you can swiftly address these issues and keep your kids smiling and ready to embrace each new adventure.

Maintaining a healthy diet and hydration during the trip:
A well-nourished and hydrated child is a happy and energized traveler. Encourage your school-age kids to embrace a balanced diet during your

journey. Introduce them to local culinary delights while ensuring they consume a variety of fruits, vegetables, and whole grains. Hydration is also vital, so pack refillable water bottles and encourage regular water intake throughout the day. Balancing indulgences with nutritious choices will keep your little ones fueled for all the incredible experiences that lie ahead.

Childproofing Your Travel Environment

Safety considerations for accommodations:

When choosing accommodations, prioritize safety features that cater to your kids' needs. Look for properties that offer childproofing measures such as outlet covers, corner guards, and stair gates. Ensure that windows have secure locks or child proof window stops. Additionally, check for smoke detectors, fire extinguishers, and emergency exit routes. By selecting child-friendly accommodations, you can relax and enjoy your trip, knowing that your children are in a secure environment.

Childproofing techniques for hotel rooms and rental properties:

Even if accommodations are not specifically childproofed, you can take proactive steps to make them safer for your kids. Carry a few essential childproofing items such as outlet covers, door handle covers, and cabinet locks. Create a designated play area by removing any hazardous objects and ensuring furniture is securely anchored. Perform a thorough inspection upon arrival, identifying potential risks, and taking appropriate measures to mitigate them. With a little effort, you can transform any space into a child-friendly haven.

Ensuring a safe environment during transportation:
Traveling from one place to another often involves various modes of transportation. Prioritize your children's safety during these journeys by ensuring they wear seat belts or use appropriate child car seats. If using

public transportation, keep a close eye on your kids and have a designated meeting point in case anyone gets separated. Educate your children on general safety rules for traveling and remind them to be aware of their surroundings. By instilling these safety practices, you'll create a secure travel environment for the entire family.

Tips for navigating crowded tourist attractions with kids:

Exploring popular tourist attractions can be exhilarating, but it's essential to keep safety in mind, especially in crowded environments. Establish a designated meeting point in case anyone gets separated, and teach your children to approach security personnel or information desks if they need help. Dress your kids in bright and distinctive clothing to make them easily identifiable in a crowd. Hold hands or use child wristbands to maintain physical contact in busy areas. By employing these techniques, you'll navigate crowded attractions with confidence and peace of mind.

Emergency protocols and locating nearby medical facilities:

While nobody wants to anticipate emergencies, being prepared is crucial. Familiarize yourself with emergency protocols at your destination, such as the local emergency phone number and medical facilities. Keep a list of nearby hospitals or clinics in case immediate medical attention is required. Research local customs and practices, so you are aware of the healthcare system and how to navigate it if the need arises. By having this knowledge at your fingertips, you'll swiftly respond to any unexpected situations.

By prioritizing health essentials, being prepared for common travel-related health issues, and childproofing your travel environment, you can embark on your journey with peace of mind. Whether it's a day at a crowded attraction or a peaceful night in your accommodation, your children's safety and well-being will be safeguarded. So, fearlessly explore the world and nurture the spirit of adventure in your little explorers!

Unleash the Adventurer Within - Practical Gear for Memorable Sightseeing and Exploration!

Gear Up and Dive into Epic Discoveries!

Are you ready to embark on awe-inspiring adventures with your school-age kids? This chapter is your ultimate guide to practical gear that will enhance your sightseeing and exploration experiences. From immersing yourself in the great outdoors to discovering the hidden gems of vibrant cities, we'll explore the colorful world of gear designed to make your journeys extraordinary. So, grab your gear and let's dive into a world of excitement and discovery!

Exploring the Outdoors with Kids

Outdoor gear for hiking, camping, and nature walks:
When venturing into the great outdoors with your school-age kids, it's essential to have the right gear. Invest in sturdy and comfortable backpacks or daypacks that can carry essentials such as water bottles, snacks, extra layers, and a small first aid kit. Don't forget to pack appropriate clothing for the outdoors, including breathable and moisture-wicking fabrics, sturdy hiking boots, and rain jackets. Consider trekking poles for added stability during hikes, and ensure everyone has their own reusable water bottle to stay hydrated throughout your outdoor adventures.

Binoculars, magnifying glasses, and field guides:

Ignite your kids' curiosity and love for nature with gear that encourages exploration. Equip them with binoculars to observe wildlife from a distance, magnifying glasses to examine intricate details of plants and insects, and field guides to identify the flora and fauna you encounter. These tools will not only make your outdoor excursions educational but also provide endless entertainment and discovery for your young adventurers.

Sun protection essentials (sunscreen, hats, sunglasses):

When spending time outdoors, it's crucial to protect your family from the sun's rays. Pack a high SPF sunscreen and apply it generously to exposed skin. Don't forget to cover heads with wide-brimmed hats to shield faces and necks from the sun. Sunglasses with UV protection are a must to safeguard your children's eyes from harmful rays. By prioritizing sun protection, you can enjoy your outdoor adventures without worry.

Insect repellents and protective clothing:

When exploring nature, pesky insects can sometimes interrupt the fun. Arm yourself with effective insect repellents to keep bugs at bay. Look for formulas suitable for kids and apply as directed. Additionally, dress your kids in long-sleeved shirts, long pants, and socks to provide an extra layer of protection. Consider lightweight, breathable fabrics that also offer mosquito protection. With these measures in place, you can enjoy the beauty of nature without the nuisance of unwanted bites.

Portable seating and picnic accessories:

Make the most of your outdoor experiences by bringing along portable seating options and picnic accessories. Pack foldable camping chairs or lightweight blankets for comfortable seating during breaks or scenic viewpoints. Consider collapsible tables for convenient picnic setups. Don't forget to bring reusable water bottles, snacks, and a picnic basket filled with delicious treats to recharge and enjoy quality family time amidst nature's wonders.

Urban Adventures and City Sightseeing

Strollers and baby carriers for younger children:

When exploring cities with younger children, it's essential to have appropriate gear for their comfort and convenience. Invest in lightweight and easy-to-maneuver strollers that can handle different terrains. Consider strollers with additional features like reclining seats, sunshades, and storage compartments. Baby carriers are also great options for hands-free exploration, allowing you to navigate crowded streets and attractions with ease while keeping your little ones close and secure.

Travel-friendly maps and guidebooks:

To navigate through cities and make the most of your sightseeing adventures, arm yourself with travel-friendly maps and guidebooks. Opt for compact and foldable maps that provide detailed information on attractions, public transportation routes, and points of interest. Guidebooks tailored to family travel can offer insider tips, kid-friendly attractions, and suggested itineraries that will maximize your city explorations.

Lightweight and versatile daypacks:

When sightseeing in cities, it's crucial to have a lightweight and versatile daypack to carry your essentials. Look for backpacks with multiple compartments and adjustable straps for optimal comfort. These daypacks can hold items such as water bottles, snacks, cameras, extra layers, and souvenirs. Ensure the daypacks have sufficient room to accommodate any treasures your kids may collect along the way.

Navigating public transportation with kids:

Getting around in cities often involves public transportation. Familiarize yourself with the local transportation system and plan your routes in advance. Consider obtaining travel passes or cards that offer unlimited rides for a specific duration. Teach your kids about subway or bus etiquette, such as giving up seats for the elderly or pregnant individuals. Be prepared with entertainment options to keep your kids engaged during transit, such as travel games, books, or audio stories.

Comfortable walking shoes and clothing:

Exploring cities involves a lot of walking, so it's crucial to have comfortable shoes and clothing. Choose lightweight, breathable shoes with good arch support that will keep your family's feet happy and blister-free. Opt for moisture-wicking and quick-drying clothing to stay comfortable during long days of exploration. Layering options will help you adapt to changing weather conditions. Encourage your kids to express their style while keeping comfort in mind, so they can truly enjoy every step of your urban adventures.

Equipped with practical gear, you're now ready to embark on memorable sightseeing and exploration adventures with your school-age kids. From immersing yourself in the great outdoors with hiking gear and nature exploration tools to navigating city streets with strollers, maps, and comfortable footwear, the world is yours to discover. So, embrace the vibrant colors of exploration, seize the day with enthusiasm, and let your family's wanderlust guide you towards extraordinary experiences. Adventure awaits!

Chapter 5

Family-Friendly Accommodations

The Kowalski family embarked on an adventurous journey to the iconic city of San Francisco, California. With the Golden Gate Bridge in their sights, they were ready to experience the city's unique charm and breathtaking views.

Their first stop was Fisherman's Wharf, a bustling area known for its fresh seafood and vibrant atmosphere. As they strolled along the waterfront, the enticing smell of clam chowder filled the air.

Eager to taste the renowned San Francisco delicacy, little Sloane declared, "I want the biggest bowl of clam chowder in the whole world!"

With her bold proclamation, the Kowalski family ventured into a bustling seafood restaurant. They ordered a large bowl of clam chowder and eagerly awaited their culinary adventure.

When the waiter finally arrived with a gargantuan bowl, their eyes widened in disbelief. It wasn't just the largest bowl of clam chowder they had ever seen—it was practically the size of a bathtub!

The Kowalskis couldn't contain their laughter as they realized the sheer absurdity of the situation. The neighboring tables glanced over, intrigued by the family's contagious amusement.

Undeterred by the daunting challenge, Mr. Kowalski grabbed a giant ladle and made it his mission to conquer the colossal bowl of chowder. With each spoonful, he playfully exaggerated his efforts, feigning exhaustion and dramatically wiping his brow.

The kids, amused by their dad's performance, joined in on the fun, taking turns pretending to dive into the enormous bowl like synchronized swimmers. Their antics turned heads and sparked laughter from fellow diners, transforming the restaurant into an impromptu comedy club.

As the Kowalski family's laughter echoed through the restaurant, they managed to devour a significant portion of the mammoth bowl of clam chowder. The waiter, impressed by their enthusiasm, jokingly asked if they wanted a to-go container the size of a suitcase.

With full bellies and smiling faces, the Kowalskis left the restaurant with a newfound appreciation for family bonding, laughter, and their shared ability to tackle any culinary challenge.

Throughout the rest of their San Francisco adventure, the family would fondly reminisce about their epic clam chowder conquest. To this day, whenever they encounter a large serving of any dish, they jokingly refer to it as "Kowalski-sized."

The Kowalski family's escapade in San Francisco taught them the importance of embracing laughter, even in the face of daunting tasks, and the joy that comes from creating unforgettable memories together.

Picture this: you're embarking on a memorable family adventure, ready to create lasting memories with your loved ones. But before you take off, there's an important decision to make – where will you stay? Choosing the right accommodation for your family trip is like finding the perfect puzzle piece to complete your vacation masterpiece. In this section, we'll delve into the world of family-friendly accommodations, where comfort, safety, and entertainment options seamlessly come together to ensure a pleasant stay for the whole family.

Importance of choosing the right accommodation for a family trip

Selecting suitable accommodations for your family trip is more than just finding a place to sleep. It sets the foundation for a relaxing and enjoyable vacation experience. After long days of exploring, you'll want a haven where your little ones can rest and rejuvenate, allowing you to do the same. Family-friendly accommodations cater to the unique needs of families, offering a welcoming environment where everyone feels at ease and can unwind after a day of adventures.

Factors to consider when selecting family-friendly accommodations

When it comes to finding the perfect family-friendly accommodation, a few key factors can make a significant difference. Consider the size of your family and the number of bedrooms or suites required to ensure everyone has their own space. Look for accommodations that offer childproofing and safety features, such as outlet covers, stair gates, and secure windows, giving you peace of mind as your little explorers roam around.

Additionally, amenities catering specifically to families can make your stay more convenient and enjoyable. Look out for facilities like playrooms, kids' pools, and outdoor playgrounds. Some accommodations even provide cribs, high chairs, and strollers, saving you the hassle of bringing your own bulky equipment. By considering these factors, you'll be well on your way to finding a family-friendly haven that ticks all the boxes.

Benefits of staying in family-friendly accommodations

Staying in family-friendly accommodations offers a multitude of benefits that go beyond mere convenience. These establishments understand the unique dynamics of family travel and go the extra mile to ensure an unforgettable experience. From friendly and accommodating staff to thoughtful amenities, they create an atmosphere that makes families feel welcomed and valued.

Moreover, family-friendly accommodations often provide a variety of entertainment options to keep your little adventurers engaged. Imagine a hotel with a dedicated kids' club offering exciting activities and supervised play sessions, or a resort with a thrilling water park where the whole family can splash and slide to their heart's content. These experiences not only keep the children entertained but also provide opportunities for parents to relax and enjoy some well-deserved downtime.

Choosing family-friendly accommodations sets the stage for a successful family trip. These accommodations offer a blend of comfort, safety, and entertainment options, making them the perfect home away from home for your entire clan. So, let's dive in and explore the world of family-friendly accommodations, uncovering the hidden gems that will make your family vacation truly extraordinary. Get ready for a journey filled with laughter, adventure, and unforgettable memories!

Hotels and Resorts - The Ultimate Playground for School-Age Kids

Welcome to a world where family vacations are taken to a whole new level of excitement and adventure! If you're traveling with school-age kids, hotels and resorts are your golden ticket to a vacation experience filled with boundless fun and unforgettable memories. In this section, we'll explore the advantages of choosing hotels and resorts as your family's home base during your adventures.

Endless Activities and Entertainment

Hotels and resorts have perfected the art of keeping young minds and bodies engaged. They are like vibrant playgrounds, offering a plethora of activities that cater specifically to school-age kids. From splash-tastic swimming pools with water slides to action-packed sports courts, there's never a dull moment in these spirited havens.

Imagine your kids giggling with delight as they participate in treasure hunts, arts and crafts workshops, or mini-Olympic competitions organized by the hotel's energetic staff. These establishments often have dedicated kids' clubs, where children can make new friends and create memories while indulging in age-appropriate games, movies, and even themed parties. The best part? While your kids are having a blast, you can enjoy some well-deserved relaxation, knowing they are in safe and capable hands.

Family-Friendly Amenities

Hotels and resorts understand the needs of families on the go, and they go above and beyond to make your vacation as smooth as possible. School-age kids come with unique requirements, and these accommodations are well-prepared to meet them head-on.

Many hotels and resorts offer spacious family suites or interconnecting rooms, ensuring that everyone has their own space to unwind after a day of exploration. You'll find amenities like extra beds, pull-out sofas, and cribs readily available, eliminating the need to lug around bulky equipment. Some establishments even provide kid-friendly toiletries, bathrobes, and slippers to make your little ones feel extra special.

On-Site Dining Options

We all know how demanding school-age kids can be when it comes to their taste buds. Hotels and resorts have got you covered with a variety of dining options to please even the pickiest eaters. From buffet-style restaurants with a multitude of choices to themed eateries that bring joy and excitement to every meal, these accommodations offer a culinary journey that satisfies the entire family.

Moreover, many hotels and resorts provide special kids' menus with child-friendly dishes and portion sizes. Don't be surprised if your little adventurers find themselves munching on delectable treats they've never tried before. And for those with dietary restrictions or food allergies, these establishments are typically well-equipped to accommodate your needs, ensuring that everyone can savor their vacation meals to the fullest.

Hotels and resorts are like dream destinations within themselves when it comes to family vacations with school-age kids. With endless activities and entertainment, family-friendly amenities, and a diverse range of dining options, they effortlessly cater to the unique needs and desires of your young adventurers. So, get ready to dive into a world where fun knows no bounds and where every day is filled with laughter, joy, and the sheer excitement of discovery. Your family's ultimate vacation playground awaits!

Private Homes - Your Family's Personal Oasis

When it comes to family vacations with school-age kids, the phrase "home away from home" takes on a whole new meaning. Imagine having a private haven where your family can unwind, bond, and create cherished memories together. Private homes offer a unique and intimate experience that perfectly complements the dynamics of traveling with school-age kids. In this section, we'll dive into the advantages of choosing a private home as your family's vacation retreat.

Space to Spread Out and Relax

One of the greatest advantages of staying in a private home is the abundance of space it provides for your family. School-age kids thrive when they have room to roam and let their imaginations run wild. Whether it's a spacious living room, a sprawling backyard, or a cozy patio, a private home offers a personal oasis where everyone can spread out, unwind, and truly make themselves at home.

With separate bedrooms for the kids and parents, everyone can enjoy their privacy while still being under the same roof. And let's not forget about the joy of having your own kitchen! Prepare delicious home-cooked meals or let your little chefs try their hand at culinary creations. The flexibility and freedom a private home offers cannot be overstated, creating an environment where your family can relax, recharge, and make lifelong memories.

Local Experience and Cultural Immersion

Choosing a private home allows you to immerse your family in the local culture and experience your destination like a true insider. By staying in residential neighborhoods, you'll have the opportunity to interact with locals, explore hidden gems, and gain a deeper understanding of the local way of life.

Take your kids on a stroll through the neighborhood, where they can play in local parks, discover charming cafes, and even make friends with the neighbors' children. Encourage them to engage with the community, whether it's joining in a friendly game of street soccer or learning a few phrases of the local language. These experiences not only broaden their horizons but also foster a sense of curiosity and empathy for different cultures.

Flexibility and Convenience

Traveling with school-age kids often means juggling schedules, preferences, and varying energy levels. Private homes offer the flexibility and convenience to cater to your family's specific needs. With a fully equipped kitchen, you have the option to prepare meals at your own pace and accommodate individual dietary requirements. No more rushing to make it to breakfast before it ends!

Additionally, private homes often provide amenities like laundry facilities, which can be a lifesaver when it comes to keeping up with the inevitable spills and stains that come with traveling with kids. Plus, having a dedicated space to unwind, such as a backyard or a cozy living area, means you can create your own family rituals and enjoy quality time together without the distractions of a bustling hotel environment.

Choosing a private home for your family vacation opens up a world of possibilities. The space, comfort, and flexibility it offers create a personal oasis for your school-age kids to relax and thrive. Embrace the local culture, immerse yourselves in the community, and enjoy the convenience of a home away from home. Get ready to embark on a journey where every day is filled with adventure and the magic of discovering new horizons alongside your loved ones. Your family's private retreat awaits!

Chapter 6

Cultural Immersion - Expanding Horizons Through Local Experiences

The Airy family embarked on a thrilling adventure to the bustling city of Tokyo, Japan. With their passports in hand and hearts full of excitement, they were ready to immerse themselves in the unique culture and vibrant atmosphere of the city.

Their first stop was the iconic Shibuya Crossing, a bustling intersection famous for its crowds of people and towering billboards. As they stood on the sidewalk, the kids, Lily and Ethan, watched in awe as the traffic lights changed, and a wave of people surged across the intersection.

Feeling a surge of bravery, Lily turned to her parents with determination in her eyes. "I want to lead the way and cross the street first," she declared, determined to experience the thrill of navigating the famous Shibuya Crossing.

The Airy family chuckled, amused by Lily's determination, and agreed to let her take the lead. As the lights changed, Lily, with her head held high, confidently stepped onto the busy crosswalk, her family following closely behind.

But as they made their way across the intersection, Ethan noticed that his shoelace had come undone. In a panic, he bent down to tie it, completely oblivious to the sea of people flowing around him.

Realizing her brother's predicament, Lily, being the protective big sister, quickly grabbed Ethan's hand and expertly weaved through the crowd, carefully avoiding collisions with other pedestrians.

The Airy parents, momentarily separated from their kids, watched with bated breath as Lily skillfully navigated the chaos, keeping Ethan safe by her side. It was like witnessing a mini superheroine in action.

Finally, Lily guided Ethan to safety on the opposite side of the street, triumphantly turning to her parents with a smile that lit up the entire intersection. The Airy family reunited, bursting into applause and laughter, receiving amused glances from passersby.

As they continued their Tokyo adventure, the Airy family would lovingly refer to Lily as their "Shibuya Navigator," forever cherishing the memory of her bravery and her determination to protect her little brother amidst the bustling crowds.

Their trip to Tokyo taught the Airy family the importance of looking out for one another and the power of sibling love. It became a reminder that even in the midst of busy and unfamiliar places, their bond as a family would always guide them safely through any journey.

Welcome to an extraordinary adventure, where the world becomes your classroom and cultural immersion is the key to unlocking a treasure trove of unforgettable experiences. In this travel book, we embark on a thrilling journey tailored for families with school-age children, as we delve into the wonders of traveling with a purpose: to expand horizons through local experiences and create lifelong memories.

Importance of cultural immersion for children's development:

As parents, we yearn for our children to grow into compassionate, open-minded individuals who appreciate the diverse tapestry of humanity. Cultural immersion plays a pivotal role in shaping their development by fostering a deep understanding and respect for different customs, traditions, and languages. It provides a unique opportunity for our young adventurers to witness firsthand the beauty and intricacies of cultures around the globe.

Benefits of experiencing different customs, traditions, and languages:

Imagine your children's eyes lighting up with wonder as they participate in a traditional dance, learn to craft intricate artwork, or savor the flavors of a local delicacy. By engaging in these diverse experiences, they gain a broader perspective, cultivating empathy, tolerance, and a global mindset. Through cultural immersion, they become citizens of the world, eager to embrace the richness and complexity of our planet's tapestry.

Setting expectations and creating a positive mindset for cultural immersion

As we embark on this remarkable journey, it is essential to set the stage for a transformative experience. Together, we will discover how to create a positive mindset that embraces the unknown, embraces differences, and celebrates the joy of connecting with people from all walks of life. We will guide you in managing expectations, nurturing curiosity, and fostering a sense of adventure that will make each cultural encounter a gateway to personal growth and family bonding.

So, get ready to step off the beaten path, to wander through bustling markets, taste exotic flavors, and breathe in the vibrant spirit of new lands. Join us as we unlock the secrets of cultural immersion, uncover hidden gems, and create cherished memories that will forever shape the hearts and minds of your children.

Welcome to the gateway of cultural immersion! Before we embark on this exhilarating journey with your family, let's take a moment to prepare for the kaleidoscope of experiences that await us. As we delve into the vibrant tapestry of customs, traditions, and languages, we'll equip you with the tools and knowledge to navigate these new horizons with ease and grace.

Learning about the local customs, traditions, and etiquette

Imagine the joy on your child's face as they join in a traditional dance or engage in a local custom. Understanding the cultural nuances of your destination is like opening a treasure chest of authentic experiences. From learning to greet locals with a warm smile and a few simple phrases, to understanding proper etiquette at religious sites or during mealtime, we'll guide you in embracing the rich tapestry of traditions that make each culture unique.

Basic language phrases and useful vocabulary for interacting with locals

Language is the key that unlocks doors to meaningful connections. While fluency may take time, learning a few basic phrases can work wonders in bridging cultural gaps and fostering genuine interactions. We'll teach you the essential words and phrases for greetings, expressions of gratitude, and simple conversations. Witness the delight on your child's face as they proudly communicate with locals, building bridges of understanding and forging friendships that transcend borders.

Packing essentials for cultural experiences

As we embark on this cultural odyssey, it's important to be prepared with the right tools. Packing appropriately not only shows respect for the local customs but also enhances your family's comfort and enjoyment. From lightweight, breathable clothing that respects local modesty norms to comfortable walking shoes for exploring vibrant markets, we'll ensure you have everything you need for your immersive adventures. Additionally, we'll introduce you to essential translation tools, apps, or phrase books that will aid in overcoming language barriers and make your interactions smoother than ever.

Picture yourselves strolling through bustling bazaars, adorned in colorful attire, greeting locals with confidence, and immersing yourselves in the vibrant rhythm of a foreign land. Your family will be a shining example of cultural curiosity and respect, embracing the traditions and languages of the places you visit.

So pack your bags with a sense of wonder and anticipation, and prepare to embark on an extraordinary journey. Together, we'll unlock the secrets of cultural immersion, immersing your family in a world of captivating customs, traditions, and languages. Get ready to create memories that will leave an indelible mark on your hearts and minds forever. Let the adventure begin!

Welcome to a world where authenticity reigns supreme! As we journey together in search of immersive experiences for your family, let's dive headfirst into the kaleidoscope of local wonders that await us. Get ready to peel back the layers and uncover the true essence of your destination through vibrant markets, jubilant festivals, and heartfelt connections with the local communities.

Exploring local markets and street vendors

Step into a realm of tantalizing aromas, vibrant colors, and the lively hum of local life. Local markets and street vendors are veritable treasure troves of authentic experiences, where your family can engage with the heartbeat of a destination. Join the rhythm of bargaining, taste exotic fruits and delectable street food, and marvel at the craftsmanship of local artisans. From vibrant textiles to intricate handicrafts, these markets offer a glimpse into the soul of the community, allowing you to take a piece of it home with you.

Participating in cultural festivals, celebrations, and events

Immerse yourself in a whirlwind of festivities and joyous celebrations! Cultural festivals and events provide a gateway to the heart and soul of a community. From colorful parades to traditional dances and mesmerizing performances, these vibrant spectacles ignite the imagination and leave indelible memories for your family. Participate in time-honored rituals, don traditional attire, and let the infectious energy of the festivities engulf you. By joining these celebrations, you become an honorary member of the community, forging connections that transcend language and culture.

Connecting with local communities through volunteering or homestays

The true essence of cultural immersion lies in forging authentic connections with the people who call your destination home. Engaging in volunteer work or opting for a homestay experience allows your family to experience the destination from within, embracing the everyday lives of locals. From participating in community projects to sharing meals and stories with your host family, these experiences will deepen your understanding of the local culture and foster genuine bonds. Your children will witness the power of giving back, as they contribute to meaningful causes and gain a newfound appreciation for the world around them.

Imagine your family strolling through bustling markets, exchanging laughter with street vendors, dancing alongside locals in colorful festivals, and forming lifelong friendships with people who initially felt like strangers. These authentic experiences will leave an imprint on your hearts and souls, shaping your understanding of the world and igniting a curiosity that will last a lifetime.

So, let your spirits soar as you embark on this quest for authenticity. Open your hearts and minds to the beauty of local markets, festivals, and communities, as you become part of a tapestry woven with the threads of shared experiences. Get ready to create memories that will forever carry the vibrant spirit of the places you visit. The adventure awaits, and it's time to immerse yourselves in the authentic wonders of the world!

Feed Your Soul with Local Cuisine

Prepare your taste buds for a gastronomic journey like no other! As we explore the world through a culinary lens, we invite your family to savor the flavors, indulge in delectable dishes, and embark on unforgettable food adventures. Get ready to tantalize your senses, expand your palates, and create delicious memories together.

Discovering local cuisine and traditional dishes

Imagine the aromas that waft through the air, drawing you into a world of culinary wonders. Each destination has a unique tapestry of flavors waiting to be discovered. From aromatic spices and mouth watering street food to sumptuous traditional dishes passed down through generations, your family will embark on a delightful exploration of local cuisine. Dive into vibrant markets, visit bustling food stalls, and seek out hidden gems recommended by locals. Every bite will be a window into the culture, a way to connect with the heart and soul of your destination.

Engaging in cooking classes and food tours

Unleash your inner chef as you step into the kitchen! Engaging in cooking classes is a fantastic way to learn the secrets of traditional recipes while bonding as a family. Under the guidance of expert chefs, your children will have the opportunity to knead dough, chop ingredients, and create mouthwatering dishes from scratch. These immersive experiences will not only provide you with new skills but also deepen your understanding of local culinary traditions. Additionally, food tours led by passionate guides will take you on a flavorful journey, introducing you to the hidden culinary gems of your destination.

Encouraging children to try new foods and flavors

Food is not just sustenance; it is an adventure waiting to be devoured! Encouraging your children to step out of their culinary comfort zones will unlock a world of exciting flavors. From exotic fruits and unique spices to unfamiliar textures and bold combinations, embracing new foods fosters a sense of openness and curiosity. Watch their faces light up as they try a dish they've never encountered before, expanding their palates and broadening their horizons. These culinary adventures will create memories that will linger on their taste buds long after you return home.

Picture yourselves sharing laughter around a table, sampling exotic dishes, and engaging in lively conversations with locals. The joy of discovering new tastes, the thrill of culinary exploration, and the bonding experiences shared over a meal will forge memories that will last a lifetime.

So, pack your appetite for adventure and get ready to feast on the flavors of the world. Let the aromas guide you, the flavors enchant you, and the shared experiences bring your family closer. From street food to fine dining, culinary traditions will become the gateway to understanding the heart and soul of your destination. Bon appétit, and let the culinary adventures begin!

The Art of Cultural Immersion with your Family

Prepare to unleash your family's creative spirits as we embark on a journey into the vibrant world of arts, crafts, and traditional skills! From the stroke of a paintbrush to the mastery of intricate crafts, this chapter will ignite your imagination, awaken your senses, and leave you in awe of the artistic heritage of your destination.

Engaging in local art workshops and classes

Step into the realm of creativity as you and your children immerse yourselves in local art workshops and classes. Unleash your inner artists as you learn techniques passed down through generations. Paint vibrant landscapes, sculpt clay into magnificent shapes, or weave intricate textiles under the guidance of talented artisans. These workshops provide a hands-on experience, allowing your family to express yourselves artistically while connecting with the local culture. Watch as your children's faces light up with joy and pride as they create unique masterpieces inspired by the rich tapestry of their surroundings.

Learning traditional crafts and skills from local artisans

Witness the magic of craftsmanship as you learn traditional crafts and skills from local artisans. Immerse yourself in the world of handmade wonders as you discover the secrets of pottery, woodworking, basket weaving, or traditional fabric dyeing. Engage in conversations with artisans, unraveling the stories behind their creations, and gain insight into their time-honored techniques. These encounters provide a window into the cultural heritage of your destination, and the skills you acquire will become cherished keepsakes that you can pass down through generations.

Experiencing performances, music, and dance unique to the culture

Let the rhythm of the local culture guide your feet and ignite your spirits as you experience performances, music, and dance unique to your destination. Immerse yourself in captivating melodies, witness spellbinding dance performances, and let the energy of traditional music envelop your senses. From toe-tapping beats to graceful movements, these performances showcase the artistic traditions that have shaped the identity of the community. Engage in interactive workshops where you and your children can learn basic steps, try traditional instruments, or even participate in a performance. The joy of cultural expression will create lasting memories and leave you with a deep appreciation for the performing arts.

Imagine your family immersed in a world of colors, textures, and creative expressions. From painting vibrant canvases to crafting intricate objects, and from witnessing breathtaking performances to joining in rhythmic dances, your journey through arts, crafts, and traditional skills will ignite your imagination and inspire you to see the world through a new lens.

So, let your creativity soar as you dive into the world of artistic wonders. Embrace the opportunity to learn from talented artisans, celebrate the beauty of local craftsmanship, and let the performances and dances transport you to a world of enchantment. The adventure awaits – unleash your inner artist and let your family's creative spirits shine!

Museums, Landmarks, and History, oh my!

Get ready to embark on a captivating journey through time as we explore the historical and cultural sites that have shaped the tapestry of our world! From ancient wonders to modern marvels, this chapter invites your family to delve into the depths of history, unlocking the stories and secrets hidden within these remarkable landmarks.

Visiting museums, historical landmarks, and UNESCO World Heritage sites

Step into a world where the past comes alive and the echoes of history reverberate through the corridors of time. Museums will open their doors, offering glimpses into the lives of those who came before us. Historical landmarks will stand tall, bearing witness to the triumphs and struggles of civilizations long gone. UNESCO World Heritage sites will enchant you with their universal value and outstanding cultural significance. From awe-inspiring castles to ancient ruins and architectural wonders, these sites will transport you back in time, providing a window into the heritage of your destination.

Understanding the historical significance of the destination

Immerse yourself in the stories that have shaped the identity of the places you visit. Understanding the historical significance of your destination will unlock a deeper appreciation for its culture, traditions, and people. Unravel the tales of empires, revolutions, and cultural movements that have left an indelible mark on the landscape. Dive into the history books, engage with knowledgeable guides, and allow the stories to transport you to a bygone era. Through understanding, you and your children will develop a profound connection to the destination and its heritage.

Encouraging children to ask questions and engage in discussions

Ignite the spirit of curiosity in your children as you explore historical and cultural sites. Encourage them to ask questions, ponder the significance of what they see, and engage in discussions. Let their imaginations run wild as they envision the lives of those who walked these streets centuries ago. These conversations will foster critical thinking, empathy, and a deeper understanding of the world around them. Encourage them to reflect on the similarities and differences between past and present, sparking conversations that will broaden their perspectives and enrich their cultural understanding.

Picture your family standing in awe before ancient monuments, tracing the footsteps of historical figures, and delving into the depths of human history. These explorations will ignite a lifelong curiosity for the past, leaving an indelible mark on the minds and hearts of your children.

So, let the allure of history draw you in as you explore the historical and cultural sites that grace our world. Marvel at the wonders of the past, unravel the stories that lie within these remarkable landmarks, and ignite the flame of curiosity in your children. The adventure awaits – step into the annals of time and let history unfold before your eyes!

Make Local Connections

Get ready to open your hearts and forge lifelong connections as we dive into the beautiful tapestry of human connections through connecting with local families! In this chapter, we invite your family to embrace the warmth, hospitality, and unique perspectives of local communities. Through playdates, shared meals, and a glimpse into everyday life, you'll create bonds that transcend borders and create lasting memories.

Arranging playdates or cultural exchanges with local children
Unlock the universal language of play and watch as your children's laughter intertwines with that of local kids. Arrange playdates or cultural exchanges, allowing your little adventurers to engage in games, sports, and activities that bridge cultural differences. Through shared experiences, they'll discover that the joy of childhood transcends language barriers and cultural boundaries. Witness the magic of friendships forming, as they learn from one another, exchange stories, and create bonds that stretch across continents.

Sharing meals or hosting a meal with a local family

Prepare to tantalize your taste buds and nourish your souls as you share a meal with local families. Whether dining at their table or hosting them in your temporary home, the breaking of bread together is a universal symbol of connection. Savor traditional dishes, sipping flavors that reflect the essence of their culture. Engage in heartfelt conversations, sharing stories, and learning about one another's lives.

Through the experience of food and hospitality, you'll create memories that will forever bind your families together.

Experiencing everyday life through the eyes of local families

Embrace the opportunity to step out of the tourist bubble and experience the rhythm of everyday life through the eyes of local families. Immerse yourselves in their customs, traditions, and daily routines. From joining them in household chores to participating in local festivals or celebrations, you'll gain insight into their way of life and deepen your understanding of their culture. Witness the simplicity and beauty of everyday moments, discovering the shared values that unite us all as human beings.

Picture your family laughing with newfound friends, sharing stories over a home-cooked meal, and discovering the world through the eyes of local families. These connections will leave an indelible mark on your hearts, expanding your understanding of different cultures and reminding you of the kindness and compassion that binds us as a global community.

So, let the spirit of connection guide you as you embark on this chapter of your journey. Embrace the opportunity to create bridges of friendship, to break bread with strangers who become family, and to experience the beauty of everyday life through the eyes of locals. The adventure awaits – open your hearts, embrace the connections, and let the bonds of friendship weave their magic!

Challenges and Overcoming Cultural Barriers

Embarking on a journey of cultural immersion is an adventure that may bring its fair share of challenges, but fear not! In this chapter, we'll guide your family through the art of overcoming cultural barriers, turning obstacles into opportunities for growth and understanding. Get ready to embrace the unfamiliar, navigate communication challenges, and foster a spirit of openness and learning.

Dealing with language barriers and communication challenges

As you venture into new lands, you may encounter the delightful hurdle of language barriers. But fear not, for communication goes beyond words! Embrace the power of gestures, smiles, and the universal language of kindness. Learn a few essential phrases in the local language and be open to trying your best to communicate. The joy lies in the effort, and you'll be amazed at the connections you can forge through non-verbal communication. Embrace the opportunity to learn from locals, listen intently, and celebrate the beauty of diverse languages and expressions.

Addressing potential cultural misunderstandings or sensitivities

Cultural differences are an invitation to broaden our perspectives, but they can also present challenges. Approach potential cultural misunderstandings or sensitivities with grace and curiosity. Educate yourselves about local customs, traditions, and social norms before your journey. Respect local customs, dress codes, and traditions, always remembering to ask for permission before taking photographs, visiting sacred sites, or participating in cultural rituals. Be open to learning from your mistakes, and when in doubt, observe and follow the lead of locals. Cultivating cultural sensitivity is a continuous journey, and your willingness to learn will be appreciated by the communities you visit.

Embracing the unfamiliar and learning from challenging experiences

The unfamiliar can be intimidating, but it is also the gateway to personal growth and transformation. Embrace the unknown with open arms, for it is in moments of discomfort that we discover our true resilience and adaptability. Encourage your children to step out of their comfort zones, to try new foods, engage with unfamiliar customs, and explore uncharted territories. Embrace the beauty of cultural contrasts, seeing them as opportunities to expand your understanding of the world and learn from challenging experiences. Remember, it's in the face of the unknown that the most memorable and transformative moments await.

As you navigate the challenges and overcome cultural barriers, your family will emerge stronger, more compassionate, and with hearts open to the world. Embrace the opportunity to learn, grow, and celebrate the diversity of our planet. The challenges you encounter will become the stepping stones to a deeper connection with the places and people you encounter.

So, let your spirit of adventure shine as you navigate the path of cultural immersion. Embrace the hurdles with curiosity and grace, celebrate the differences that make our world vibrant, and emerge from the challenges stronger and wiser. The adventure awaits – let's conquer cultural barriers together!

Chapter 7

Outdoor Adventures - Embracing Nature's Playground

The Jackson family embarked on a thrilling white water rafting adventure on the majestic Snake River. With their life jackets securely fastened and paddles in hand, they were ready to tackle the exhilarating rapids as a team.

Their guide, an experienced river enthusiast, gave them a safety briefing and emphasized the importance of working together to navigate the twists and turns of the river. Mr. and Mrs. Jackson exchanged excited glances, while their three children, Peyton, Noah, and Olivia, eagerly listened, their eyes shining with anticipation.

As they set off, the first rapid loomed ahead, causing a mix of nervousness and excitement in the family. They braced themselves, ready to conquer the mighty waves. But as their raft approached the rapid, an unexpected twist occurred.

Noah, the middle child known for his clumsiness, accidentally dropped his paddle into the water. With a splash, it floated away downstream, leaving Noah wide-eyed and paddle-less.

The Jackson family erupted into laughter as Noah looked on in mock panic. Mrs. Jackson turned to him with a grin and said, "Looks like it's 'No Paddle Noah' for the rest of the ride!"

Undeterred by the paddle mishap, Mr. Jackson, quick to improvise, instructed Noah to grab onto his paddle while he controlled both his and Noah's paddles. The family marveled at their makeshift teamwork, with Noah holding on tightly to his dad's paddle, providing an extra boost of strength during each paddle stroke.

As they maneuvered through the rapids, the Jacksons couldn't help but notice the contagious laughter and joy echoing through the raft. Their synchronized paddling, along with Noah's unique paddle-holding technique, became a testament to their resilience and ability to adapt in the face of unexpected challenges.

Throughout the exhilarating ride, they shared triumphant shouts, cheering each other on as they successfully conquered rapid after rapid. The feeling of triumph washed over them, reinforcing their strong bond as a family.

When the raft finally reached calm waters, they exchanged high-fives and hugs, basking in the glow of their shared accomplishment. It wasn't just about conquering the rapids; it was about the laughter, the teamwork, and the indomitable spirit that they had discovered along the way.

As the Jackson family returned to shore, they walked away from the river with a newfound appreciation for each other and the incredible strength that comes from working together. And although Noah remained "No Paddle Noah" for the day, he became a symbol of resilience and the unwavering spirit that can transform unexpected setbacks into unforgettable moments of connection and laughter.

Welcome to a chapter bursting with vibrant adventures and thrilling escapades! In this chapter, we embark on a journey that will ignite the imaginations of your school-age children and ignite a sense of wonder within your entire family. Step into the world of outdoor activities and discover the magic that lies within nature's playground.

You may wonder, why are outdoor activities so crucial for our children? Well, dear wanderers, the benefits are as abundant as the colors of a rainbow! Engaging in outdoor adventures allows our little ones to break free from the confines of screens and concrete, immersing themselves in the natural world. It's an opportunity for them to stretch their legs, breathe in fresh air, and embrace the boundless wonders that await.

But the marvels of exploring nature are not limited to the young ones alone. Oh no! As a family, you can share in the excitement, creating memories that will forever be etched in your hearts. Picture yourselves hiking through majestic mountains, hand in hand, marveling at the breathtaking vistas. Envision the joy on your children's faces as they snorkel in crystal-clear waters, their eyes widening in amazement at the vibrant underwater world. These moments, dear adventurers, are the ones that will be cherished for a lifetime.

Now, let us unveil the treasures that lie within this chapter. We have meticulously curated a tapestry of outdoor activities that cater to families with school-age children. From invigorating hikes along scenic trails to camping in the heart of the wilderness, we have thoughtfully crafted an array of experiences to suit all tastes and preferences.

But that's not all! Prepare to dive into the depths of underwater exploration, as we guide you to the most awe-inspiring snorkeling spots. Delve into the joys of kayaking and canoeing, gliding through serene waters as a family united by adventure. And fear not, wildlife enthusiasts, for we shall lead you to encounters with magnificent creatures in zoos, national parks, and wildlife reserves.

But let us not forget the thrill-seekers and the young ones with boundless energy! Adventure parks and outdoor playgrounds await, brimming with zip lines, climbing walls, and obstacle courses that will make your hearts race with excitement.

As we embark on this chapter together, we will also delve into the importance of nature conservation and environmental awareness. Teaching our children to cherish and protect the environment is an invaluable lesson that will shape their future as responsible global citizens.

So, dear explorers, fasten your seatbelts and prepare for an exhilarating journey through the wonders of the great outdoors. Pack your enthusiasm, curiosity, and a dash of courage, for this chapter promises to be a kaleidoscope of memories, laughter, and pure joy. The adventure awaits!

Hiking Trails and Nature Walks

Step into a world of natural wonders as we venture along hiking trails and nature walks, where every step reveals breathtaking beauty and endless discoveries. This section is dedicated to families with school-age children, as we unveil the secrets of choosing trails suitable for different ages, offer tips for a well-prepared adventure, and unveil family-friendly hiking spots that will leave you in awe of nature's artistry.

As you embark on a hiking adventure with your little explorers, it's essential to select trails that cater to their abilities and interests. Fear not, for we have curated a collection of trails suitable for children of different ages. From gentle paths meandering through lush meadows to more moderate routes weaving through forests, there is something to captivate every young adventurer's imagination.

Now, let us turn our attention to preparation, as every successful hiking expedition relies on proper planning and packing. First and foremost, ensure you have an ample supply of water to keep everyone hydrated throughout the journey. Hydration is key to fueling those tiny legs and keeping spirits high. Next, let's not forget the power of snacks! Pack a variety of delicious treats that will provide sustenance and keep hunger at bay. Trail mix, energy bars, and fresh fruit are excellent options for fueling those little bodies.

Ah, footwear, the unsung heroes of hiking! It's imperative to equip your family with appropriate footwear to ensure comfort and safety. Opt for sturdy and comfortable hiking shoes that provide good ankle support and grip. Little feet need protection as they traverse various terrains, so choose wisely, dear hikers!

Now, it's time to unveil the hidden gems of family-friendly hiking spots, where captivating landscapes await your eager eyes. Picture hiking through dense forests, where sunlight filters through the canopy, illuminating the forest floor with dappled light. Imagine walking alongside babbling brooks, their soothing sounds creating a symphony of tranquility. Prepare to be amazed as you stumble upon panoramic viewpoints, revealing sweeping vistas that stretch as far as the eye can see.

In our guide, you'll find a myriad of family-friendly hiking spots, each with its unique charm and allure. Explore trails that wind through rolling hills, granting glimpses of grazing deer and colorful wildflowers. Traverse paths that lead to hidden waterfalls, their cascading waters providing a refreshing respite from the summer heat. Discover trails that lead to hidden caves or ancient ruins, where tales of bygone eras whisper through the air.

Some trail recommendations for families with school age kids:

1. Lower Yosemite Falls Trail, Yosemite National Park, California: This easy 1-mile trail takes you to the base of Lower Yosemite Falls, where

children can marvel at the thunderous cascades. Enjoy the misty spray and the breathtaking views of one of America's most iconic waterfalls.

2. Hidden Lake Trail, Glacier National Park, Montana: A family-friendly 2.7-mile round trip trail that leads to the stunning Hidden Lake. Along the way, encounter wildlife such as mountain goats and enjoy panoramic views of snow-capped mountains and alpine meadows.

3. Trail of Ten Falls, Silver Falls State Park, Oregon: This 7.2-mile loop trail showcases ten magnificent waterfalls, making it a true wonderland for children. Walk behind some of the falls and experience the magic of nature up close in this lush and picturesque forest.

4. South Kaibab Trail, Grand Canyon National Park, Arizona: While the entire trail may be challenging, the first section offers breathtaking views of the Grand Canyon. Descend down this well-maintained trail for about 1.5 miles to Ooh Aah Point, providing an unforgettable experience for the whole family.

5. Franconia Ridge Loop, White Mountains National Forest, New Hampshire: Offering spectacular views and a moderate challenge, this 8.5-mile loop trail takes you across the ridge with stunning vistas of the surrounding peaks, including Mount Lafayette. Suitable for older children who are up for a bit of adventure.

6. Delicate Arch Trail, Arches National Park, Utah: A 3-mile round trip hike to the iconic Delicate Arch, this trail leads through a stunning desert landscape. Witness the arch's magnificence and enjoy panoramic views of the red rock formations that make this park a natural wonderland.

7. Avalanche Lake Trail, Glacier National Park, Montana: A 4.5-mile round trip trail that leads to the picturesque Avalanche Lake. Children will be enchanted by the crystal-clear waters, surrounded by towering mountains and lush forests. Keep an eye out for wildlife along the way!

8. Grotto Falls Trail, Great Smoky Mountains National Park, Tennessee: A 2.6-mile round trip trail that leads to a stunning waterfall you can walk behind. The trail offers a cool and shaded pathway, perfect for a family hike on a hot summer day. Keep your cameras ready for beautiful photo opportunities.

9. Sand Beach Trail, Acadia National Park, Maine: A short and easy 0.5-mile trail that takes you to the pristine Sand Beach. Children can play in the sand and dip their toes in the refreshing Atlantic Ocean while surrounded by the rugged beauty of Acadia's coastline.

10. Skyline Trail, Mount Rainier National Park, Washington: While the full 5.5-mile loop may be more suitable for older children, the first section of this trail provides awe-inspiring views of Mount Rainier. The trail offers wildflower meadows, alpine vistas, and a chance to witness the grandeur of this majestic peak.

These hiking trails across the United States offer a range of experiences for families with school-age children, from easy strolls to more challenging adventures. Remember to check the specific trail conditions and prepare accordingly before embarking on your journey.

As you venture along these trails, keep an eye out for educational opportunities that will enhance your family's hiking experience. Some trails may have interpretive signs or educational programs that introduce children to the local flora and fauna. Encourage your young adventurers to engage with their surroundings, sparking curiosity and a deeper appreciation for the natural world.

Remember, dear explorers, hiking trails and nature walks offer more than just physical exercise. They provide opportunities for bonding as a family, for engaging in meaningful conversations while surrounded by the wonders of nature. So, lace up those hiking shoes, pack your backpacks, and get ready to embark on a journey that will both invigorate and inspire. The trails await, and adventure beckons!

Pitch your tent

Step into the realm of adventure as we venture into the wilderness, immersing ourselves in the wonders of camping. In this section, we will unlock the secrets to a successful camping trip with your school-age children, ensuring an unforgettable experience under the starry night sky. We'll provide a guide to essential camping gear and equipment, and reveal some hand-picked campgrounds that offer kid-friendly amenities and activities, making your camping escapade a delightful and memorable affair.

First and foremost, let's dive into the world of camping with school-age children, for it presents a gateway to create cherished memories and forge a deep connection with nature. Camping allows children to embrace a world free from modern distractions, where they can unplug and reconnect with their adventurous spirit. It's a chance to learn survival skills, ignite their imagination, and develop a profound appreciation for the great outdoors.

To embark on a successful camping trip, you must be equipped with the right gear and equipment. Picture a colorful array of tents, sleeping bags, and camping essentials that will transform your campsite into a cozy home away from home. Don't forget to pack a sturdy and spacious tent to accommodate your family comfortably. Sleeping bags with colorful patterns and comfortable insulation will ensure a restful night's sleep. And let us not overlook the importance of camping chairs, lanterns, and cooking utensils to elevate your camping experience.

Now, let us unveil a selection of campgrounds that cater to families with school-age children, offering a treasure trove of kid-friendly amenities and activities. These campgrounds are havens of adventure, where children can unleash their energy and explore the natural wonders that surround them.

Imagine a campground with nature-themed playgrounds, where children can climb, swing, and slide to their heart's content. Or envision a campsite nestled by a pristine lake, where little ones can dip their toes in the cool water, build sandcastles, and paddle in canoes. Some campgrounds even boast mini-golf courses, biking trails, and organized nature walks, providing endless entertainment for the young and young at heart.

Additionally, keep an eye out for campgrounds that offer interactive programs tailored specifically for children. These may include guided hikes, wildlife education, and storytelling around the campfire. Such experiences create lasting memories, inspire curiosity, and nurture a deep appreciation for the natural world.

As you embark on your camping adventure, remember to embrace the beauty of simplicity. Let your children's imaginations run wild as they explore the wonders of nature, build forts, and engage in storytelling under the starlit sky. Encourage them to participate in setting up camp, gathering firewood, and cooking simple meals over the campfire. These simple tasks foster independence, self-reliance, and a sense of pride in their contributions to the family's camping experience.

So, dear adventurers, pack your sense of wonder, a spirit of adventure, and a dash of curiosity as you prepare to embark on a camping trip with your school-age children. With essential gear in tow and our hand-picked campgrounds awaiting your arrival, this journey promises to be a kaleidoscope of joy, exploration, and family bonding. Get ready to create memories that will be etched in your hearts forever as you immerse yourselves in the beauty of camping in the wilderness. Happy camping!

Dive deep for an incredible family adventure

Dive into the realm of water adventures, where endless excitement and unforgettable memories await your family! In this section, we'll embark on two exhilarating journeys: snorkeling in pristine waters and kayaking/canoeing adventures. Let's introduce your school-age children to the wonders of snorkeling, uncover the best spots teeming with marine life, and provide essential safety precautions and gear recommendations. Then, we'll glide through calm waters, exploring serene rivers, picturesque lakes, and captivating coastal areas by kayak or canoe. Get ready to immerse yourselves in these colorful and thrilling water escapades!

First, let's plunge into the vibrant world of snorkeling and discover its many benefits for children. Picture your little ones donning snorkel masks and immersing themselves in an underwater wonderland. Snorkeling awakens a sense of awe and curiosity as children witness the incredible marine ecosystem up close. It introduces them to the diversity of ocean life, fostering a love and appreciation for the beauty and fragility of our aquatic world.

Now, let's uncover the hidden gems—the best snorkeling spots where abundant marine life and crystal-clear waters await. Imagine snorkeling amidst coral reefs, surrounded by a kaleidoscope of tropical fish. From the dazzling coral gardens of the Great Barrier Reef to the vibrant underwater world of the Maldives, these snorkeling destinations promise unforgettable encounters with marine wonders.

Ten of the best snorkeling destinations for families:

1. Hanauma Bay, Hawaii, USA: Hanauma Bay is a beautiful marine preserve on the island of Oahu, renowned for its calm, clear waters teeming with colorful fish and vibrant coral reefs. It offers a safe and

family-friendly snorkeling experience, complete with lifeguards, educational exhibits, and a shallow beach entry perfect for kids.

2. Great Barrier Reef, Australia: The Great Barrier Reef is a UNESCO World Heritage Site and the largest coral reef system in the world. With an array of snorkeling sites catering to different skill levels, families can explore this underwater wonderland together. From the Whitsunday Islands to the Outer Reef, children can discover an abundance of marine life, including turtles, tropical fish, and mesmerizing coral formations.

3. Buck Island, U.S. Virgin Islands: Buck Island is a National Monument located off the coast of St. Croix in the U.S. Virgin Islands. Its protected waters boast a pristine coral reef known as the "Underwater Trail." Families can snorkel along the trail's marked path, which provides educational signs highlighting the diverse marine ecosystem and its inhabitants.

4. Tulum, Mexico: Tulum, nestled along Mexico's Riviera Maya, offers a combination of stunning beaches and fascinating underwater caves known as cenotes. Snorkeling in these crystal-clear cenotes allows families to swim amidst stalactites and stalagmites while observing unique freshwater fish. In addition, Tulum's coastline features vibrant coral reefs teeming with colorful marine life.

5. Maldives: The Maldives is a tropical paradise renowned for its exquisite white-sand beaches and turquoise waters. Numerous resorts in the Maldives offer exceptional snorkeling opportunities for families, allowing them to explore vibrant coral reefs just steps away from their accommodations. The calm lagoons provide an ideal environment for children to safely observe tropical fish and even spot sea turtles.

6. Palawan, Philippines: Palawan, known for its breathtaking landscapes, is home to some of the most pristine snorkeling spots in the

Philippines. Families can venture to the Bacuit Archipelago, where the crystal-clear waters reveal an underwater world filled with colorful corals, exotic fish species, and even dugongs. El Nido and Coron are particularly popular snorkeling destinations within Palawan.

7. Bonaire, Caribbean Netherlands: Bonaire, a Dutch Caribbean island, is a haven for snorkeling enthusiasts. Its marine park boasts an impressive diversity of fish species and healthy coral reefs. Families can enjoy easy access to the underwater wonders by snorkeling right from the shoreline. The island's calm waters and shallow depths make it an ideal destination for kids to learn and explore.

8. Seychelles: The Seychelles archipelago in the Indian Ocean is renowned for its stunning beaches and rich marine biodiversity. Families can snorkel in secluded coves, discovering an array of colorful fish, sea turtles, and even gentle whale sharks. The clear, warm waters and abundant marine life make the Seychelles an unforgettable snorkeling destination for families.

9. Koh Phi Phi, Thailand: Koh Phi Phi, located in the Andaman Sea, offers a picturesque setting for snorkeling adventures. Families can explore the coral gardens near Maya Bay, made famous by the movie "The Beach," or venture to Bamboo Island, where the shallow, calm waters are ideal for young snorkelers. The vibrant marine life, including clownfish and parrotfish, adds to the allure of this tropical paradise.

10. Galapagos Islands, Ecuador: The Galapagos Islands, renowned for their unique wildlife and pristine ecosystems, also offer incredible snorkeling opportunities for families. Snorkeling alongside playful sea lions, observing marine iguanas, and encountering gentle sea turtles are just a few of the memorable experiences awaiting families in this UNESCO World Heritage Site. With the guidance of experienced naturalist guides, children can learn about the importance of

conservation while immersing themselves in the wonders of the Galapagos underwater world.

But let's not forget safety, dear adventurers! Before setting off on your snorkeling adventure, it's essential to be aware of safety precautions. Assess water conditions, including currents and potential hazards, and only snorkel in designated areas. Ensure everyone wears proper snorkeling gear, such as well-fitting masks and snorkels with dry-top mechanisms for easy breathing. Don't forget to protect against the sun's rays with reef-safe sunscreen and suitable clothing.

Now, let's shift gears and glide into the world of kayaking and canoeing adventures, where tranquility and exploration go hand in hand. Imagine navigating calm rivers, silently paddling through mirrored lakes, or exploring the rugged beauty of coastal areas. These water adventures offer a different perspective, immersing your family in the natural wonders that surround you.

When it comes to kayaking and canoeing with children, choosing the right vessel is key. Opt for stable and maneuverable kayaks or canoes that provide a secure and comfortable experience. Tandem kayaks are perfect for parents and children to paddle together, fostering teamwork and shared experiences. Choose locations suitable for beginners, with calm waters and gentle currents, ensuring a safe and enjoyable journey for all.

So, where can you embark on these kayaking and canoeing adventures? Picture gliding through the peaceful waters of Lake Tahoe, surrounded by stunning mountain vistas. Explore the intricate maze of the Florida Everglades, encountering unique wildlife along the way. Or paddle through the picturesque coastal inlets of Acadia National Park, where rugged cliffs meet the gentle lapping of the sea. These destinations offer a blend of beauty and serenity, inviting you to embark on unforgettable water explorations.

Ten of the best locals for families to kayak around the world:

1. Boundary Waters Canoe Area Wilderness, Minnesota, USA: Located on the Minnesota-Canada border, the Boundary Waters is a pristine wilderness area with more than 1,000 lakes and miles of interconnected waterways. Families can enjoy peaceful kayaking adventures, surrounded by stunning forests and the opportunity to spot wildlife such as moose and bald eagles.

2. Everglades National Park, Florida, USA: The Everglades is a unique ecosystem that offers kayaking opportunities like no other. Families can paddle through the park's mangrove tunnels, observing alligators, manatees, and a variety of bird species. With designated paddling trails and calm waters, the Everglades provides a safe and educational experience for kids.

3. San Juan Islands, Washington, USA: The San Juan Islands, located off the coast of Washington State, offer picturesque kayaking adventures suitable for families. With its calm waters and stunning scenery, families can paddle alongside seals, porpoises, and possibly even spot orca whales. The islands' charming coastal towns and accessible campsites make it an ideal destination for family-friendly kayaking trips.

4. Acadia National Park, Maine, USA: Acadia National Park features a rugged coastline dotted with numerous islands and secluded coves, providing excellent opportunities for family kayaking. Paddle along the park's rocky shores, explore sea caves, and enjoy breathtaking views of the Atlantic Ocean. Families can also combine their kayaking adventures with hiking and exploring the park's other attractions.

5. Glacier Bay National Park, Alaska, USA: Glacier Bay is a kayaker's paradise, offering a chance to paddle amidst towering glaciers, fjords,

and stunning ice formations. Families can embark on guided tours or rent kayaks to explore the park's pristine waterways, surrounded by magnificent wilderness and the possibility of encountering marine wildlife such as seals and whales.

6. Abel Tasman National Park, New Zealand: Situated on the South Island of New Zealand, Abel Tasman National Park boasts turquoise waters, golden beaches, and lush coastal forests. Families can kayak along the coastline, visiting hidden bays, spotting fur seals, and exploring the park's picturesque islands. With options for guided tours or self-guided adventures, this destination offers a memorable experience for all ages.

7. Sea of Cortez, Baja California, Mexico: The Sea of Cortez, also known as the Gulf of California, is a stunning kayaking destination offering encounters with diverse marine life. Families can paddle through calm waters, observing playful dolphins, sea turtles, and colorful fish. The region's warm climate and breathtaking desert landscapes add to the allure of this Mexican kayaking paradise.

8. Loch Lomond, Scotland: Loch Lomond, the largest freshwater loch in Scotland, provides a picturesque setting for family kayaking adventures. Surrounded by rolling hills and charming villages, families can paddle along the tranquil waters, stopping at scenic spots and even exploring some of the loch's islands. Loch Lomond's calm conditions and accessibility make it an ideal kayaking destination for families.

9. Dalmatian Coast, Croatia: The Dalmatian Coast in Croatia offers an enchanting blend of stunning turquoise waters, historic coastal towns, and hidden coves. Families can embark on kayaking trips, exploring the coastline's numerous islands and caves. The calm Adriatic Sea and beautiful scenery make this a memorable kayaking destination suitable for families with kids.

10. Ha Long Bay, Vietnam: Ha Long Bay, a UNESCO World Heritage Site, is renowned for its emerald waters and limestone karsts. Families can kayak through this breathtaking landscape, discovering hidden lagoons and floating fishing villages. The calm waters and unique rock formations create a magical kayaking experience, providing an opportunity for families to immerse themselves in the beauty of Vietnam's natural wonders.

As you embark on these water adventures, encourage your children to be present in the moment. Marvel at the vibrant fish swimming beneath the surface during snorkeling expeditions. Listen to the sounds of nature while kayaking or canoeing, observing wildlife in their natural habitats. These experiences cultivate a deep connection with nature and create lasting memories that will be cherished for years to come.

So, gather your snorkels, masks, kayaks, and canoes as you prepare for an exhilarating journey through water adventures. Dive into the underwater world, paddle through serene waters, and let the wonders of nature envelop you. Get ready for a splash of joy, a dash of awe, and a wave of excitement as you embrace these colorful and engaging water escapades with your school-age children. Let the water adventures begin!

It's a Wild Wild World Out There

Prepare to embark on a thrilling journey into the world of wildlife encounters, where incredible creatures and unforgettable experiences await! In this section, we'll explore two facets of wildlife adventures: zoos and wildlife parks, and national parks and wildlife reserves. Get ready to immerse yourselves in the wonders of the animal kingdom, discover family-friendly destinations, and gain insights into conservation efforts and responsible wildlife observation. Let's dive into this colorful and engaging exploration!

First, let's step into the realm of zoos and wildlife parks, where a world of captivating creatures awaits your family's eager eyes. These family-friendly destinations offer a blend of education, entertainment, and interactive experiences that ignite a passion for wildlife. Picture your children's faces lighting up as they come face-to-face with majestic lions, playful primates, and graceful giraffes. Zoos and wildlife parks provide a unique opportunity for children to observe and learn about a diverse range of animals from around the globe.

Alongside the awe-inspiring animal exhibits, these establishments often offer educational programs tailored for children. Imagine your little ones participating in feeding sessions, animal encounters, or even wildlife shows that reveal fascinating insights into animal behavior and conservation efforts. These interactive experiences foster a deeper understanding and appreciation for the natural world, igniting a sense of responsibility to protect and preserve it for future generations.

As you explore zoos and wildlife parks, take a moment to appreciate the conservation efforts they undertake. Many of these institutions play a crucial role in species preservation, breeding programs, and habitat restoration. By supporting these establishments, you contribute to their conservation initiatives, helping safeguard endangered species and their habitats for generations to come. It's a chance for your children to understand the importance of animal welfare and environmental stewardship.

Best zoos in for a family with kids in the US:

1. San Diego Zoo - San Diego, California: Renowned for its vast collection of animals and conservation efforts, the San Diego Zoo offers an immersive experience with its lush exhibits, including the popular Panda Trek and Elephant Odyssey. Children will delight in interactive shows and up-close encounters with diverse wildlife.

2. Bronx Zoo - Bronx, New York:One of the largest zoos in the United States, the Bronx Zoo showcases over 6,000 animals from around the world. Highlights include Tiger Mountain, Congo Gorilla Forest, and the Children's Zoo, where kids can feed and pet various animals.

3. Smithsonian's National Zoo - Washington, D.C.: Located in the nation's capital, the National Zoo is home to over 2,700 animals, including giant pandas, lions, and orangutans. Visitors can enjoy educational programs, behind-the-scenes tours, and special events throughout the year.

4. Audubon Zoo - New Orleans, Louisiana: Known for its vibrant and diverse exhibits, the Audubon Zoo offers a unique glimpse into the animal kingdom. From the award-winning Louisiana Swamp exhibit to the lively African Savanna, children can encounter animals from around the globe.

5. Henry Doorly Zoo and Aquarium - Omaha, Nebraska: Recognized as one of the world's best zoos, the Henry Doorly Zoo boasts exceptional exhibits such as the Desert Dome, Lied Jungle, and the Scott Aquarium. Kids will love the hands-on experiences at the interactive Kids' Kingdom.

6. Columbus Zoo and Aquarium - Columbus, Ohio: The Columbus Zoo is home to a wide array of animal species, including polar bears, gorillas, and manatees. With its extensive educational programs and interactive exhibits like the Asia Quest and Heart of Africa, children can explore the world's diverse wildlife.

7. Oregon Zoo - Portland, Oregon: Nestled in Washington Park, the Oregon Zoo offers a delightful experience with animals from around the globe. Highlights include the Elephant Lands, Great Northwest, and the immersive Africa Rainforest exhibit, where children can see a variety of animal species up close.

8. Memphis Zoo - Memphis, Tennessee: Known for its beautifully landscaped exhibits, the Memphis Zoo houses over 3,500 animals. Highlights include the Cat Country, Primate Canyon, and the Northwest Passage, where visitors can explore a polar bear exhibit.

9. Pittsburgh Zoo & PPG Aquarium - Pittsburgh, Pennsylvania: The Pittsburgh Zoo offers a diverse collection of animals from around the world, including elephants, tigers, and sea lions. Children can enjoy the Kids Kingdom, Safari Plaza, and educational programs such as the Zoo School and Animal Encounters.

10. San Francisco Zoo - San Francisco, California: Located near the Pacific Ocean, the San Francisco Zoo is a picturesque destination with a wide range of animal exhibits. Highlights include the African Savannah, Penguin Island, and the Children's Zoo, where kids can pet and interact with animals.

These zoos across the United States offer remarkable experiences, educational opportunities, and close encounters with fascinating creatures. Each one provides a unique setting to connect with wildlife and learn about conservation efforts. Remember to check their websites for specific exhibits, shows, and events to make the most of your visit!

Now, let's venture into the untamed wilderness of national parks and wildlife reserves, where the marvels of nature unfold before your very eyes. These protected areas offer a glimpse into the natural habitats of diverse wildlife species, giving you and your children the opportunity to observe them in their element. Imagine the thrill of spotting a majestic moose, an elusive leopard, or a soaring eagle in their natural environment.

When choosing national parks and wildlife reserves to visit with children, consider destinations that offer kid-friendly experiences. Look for guided nature walks, interpretive programs, or junior ranger activities that cater to young adventurers. These engaging opportunities allow children to learn about the ecosystems, wildlife behavior, and the importance of preserving these precious environments.

During your wildlife encounters in national parks and reserves, it's vital to observe and respect the wildlife from a safe distance. Encourage your children to use binoculars or spotting scopes to observe animals without intruding upon their natural behavior. Teach them to appreciate the beauty of wildlife from afar, avoiding actions that may disrupt their natural routines or cause stress. Remember, observing wildlife with empathy and respect ensures both their well-being and your family's safety.

Best national parks for families with children in the US:

1. Yellowstone National Park - Wyoming, Montana, Idaho: Yellowstone, the first national park in the United States, is a true gem. It boasts dramatic landscapes, including the iconic Old Faithful geyser, colorful hot springs, and the awe-inspiring Yellowstone Falls. Wildlife enthusiasts will delight in spotting grizzly bears, wolves, and herds of bison roaming freely.

2. Grand Canyon National Park - Arizona: The Grand Canyon's sheer size and breathtaking beauty make it a must-visit destination. Carved by the Colorado River, this iconic park offers mesmerizing vistas from its rim, showcasing layers of vibrant rock formations. Hiking trails and helicopter rides provide different perspectives of this natural wonder.

3. Yosemite National Park - California: Renowned for its towering granite cliffs, cascading waterfalls, and ancient giant sequoias, Yosemite National Park is a haven for outdoor enthusiasts. Highlights include the majestic Half Dome, Yosemite Falls, and the scenic Yosemite Valley. Hiking, rock climbing, and camping opportunities abound.

4. Zion National Park - Utah: Zion National Park is a paradise of red-rock canyons, towering sandstone cliffs, and serene rivers. The park offers breathtaking hikes, including the renowned Narrows, where you can walk through the Virgin River. Angels Landing and Observation Point provide stunning vistas for adventurers seeking a challenge.

5. Glacier National Park - Montana: Glacier National Park mesmerizes visitors with its glacial-carved peaks, pristine lakes, and alpine meadows. The iconic Going-to-the-Sun Road offers stunning viewpoints, while hiking trails like the Highline Trail and Grinnell Glacier Trail provide opportunities to encounter abundant wildlife and stunning vistas.

6. Rocky Mountain National Park - Colorado: A haven for nature lovers, Rocky Mountain National Park showcases majestic peaks, alpine lakes, and lush forests. Hiking trails like the Trail Ridge Road and Bear Lake offer incredible views, while wildlife such as elk and bighorn sheep roam freely throughout the park.

7. Acadia National Park - Maine: Acadia National Park mesmerizes visitors with its rugged coastline, granite peaks, and picturesque lakes. The park offers diverse recreational opportunities, including hiking, biking, and boating. Don't miss the sunrise from Cadillac Mountain, the highest peak on the East Coast of the United States.

8. Olympic National Park - Washington: Olympic National Park is a diverse wonderland with breathtaking rainforests, pristine beaches, and snow-capped mountains. Explore the Hoh Rainforest, stroll along the stunning coastline at Rialto Beach, or venture into the alpine region of Hurricane Ridge for panoramic views.

9. Everglades National Park - Florida: Everglades National Park is a unique and fragile ecosystem teeming with wildlife. Discover vast wetlands, mangrove forests, and freshwater marshes on airboat tours or

guided hikes. Keep an eye out for alligators, manatees, and a variety of bird species that call this park home.

10. Bryce Canyon National Park - Utah: Known for its otherworldly landscape of hoodoos—tall, thin rock formations—Bryce Canyon National Park offers mesmerizing views at every turn. Hike the Rim Trail to appreciate the stunning amphitheaters, or descend into the canyon on the Queen's Garden or Navajo Loop trails for an immersive experience.

These national parks in the United States showcase the diversity and natural beauty of the country. Each offers unique landscapes, outdoor activities, and opportunities to connect with nature. Explore, hike, camp, and soak in the wonders of these remarkable destinations. Remember to check park websites for visitor information, trail conditions, and permit requirements to make the most of your visit!

So, gather your enthusiasm, curiosity, and a sense of wonder as you prepare for an incredible wildlife adventure. Explore the world of zoos and wildlife parks, where interactive experiences and educational opportunities await. Then, venture into national parks and wildlife reserves, where you'll witness animals roaming freely in their natural habitats. Embrace the magic of wildlife encounters, foster a love for the animal kingdom, and inspire your children to be advocates for conservation and environmental stewardship. Let the wildlife adventures begin!

Seasonal Adventures: Embrace the Elements!

Winter Sports and Activities:
As the snowflakes begin to fall, it's time to embark on exciting winter sports and activities that will make your family's spirits soar! In this section, we'll introduce you to winter sports suitable for children, unveil family-friendly ski resorts and winter destinations, and provide essential

safety measures and equipment recommendations for a memorable snowy adventure.

Picture your children gliding down the slopes, their rosy cheeks beaming with joy as they conquer the slopes on skis or snowboards. Winter sports like skiing and snowboarding are not only exhilarating but also provide excellent opportunities for children to develop balance, coordination, and confidence. Encourage them to take lessons tailored for their age and skill level, ensuring a safe and enjoyable experience on the slopes.

Now, let's discover the best family-friendly ski resorts and winter destinations, where the magic of winter comes alive. Imagine pristine snow-covered mountains, cozy lodges with crackling fireplaces, and a plethora of activities for the whole family. Resorts like Aspen Snowmass, Park City Mountain, and Whistler Blackcomb offer a perfect blend of ski slopes, winter adventures, and accommodations suitable for families.

When venturing into winter sports and activities, safety is of utmost importance. Make sure everyone wears appropriate winter gear, including helmets, goggles, and warm clothing. Familiarize yourselves with resort safety guidelines, such as slope etiquette and designated areas for different skill levels. Stay updated on weather conditions and follow any instructions from ski patrol or resort staff for a secure and enjoyable experience on the slopes.

Summer Water Fun:

As the temperatures rise, it's time to dive into summer water fun and beat the heat with refreshing aquatic adventures! In this section, we'll introduce you to a variety of water-based activities, highlight family-friendly water parks, splash pads, and swimming spots, and provide essential water safety tips and supervision guidelines for children.

Imagine your children squealing with delight as they slide down water slides, splash in pools, and engage in thrilling water-based activities. Water parks and splash pads are havens of laughter and excitement, offering a perfect respite from the summer heat. Destinations like Schlitterbahn, Great Wolf Lodge, and Noah's Ark Waterpark provide a blend of thrilling slides, lazy rivers, and interactive play areas, ensuring endless hours of fun for the whole family.

But the adventure doesn't stop there! Seek out natural swimming spots like lakes, rivers, and beaches, where your family can enjoy a refreshing dip amidst stunning surroundings. Explore destinations like Lake Tahoe, the crystal-clear waters of the Florida Keys, or the tranquil lakes of the Adirondacks. Remember to adhere to safety guidelines and supervise your children at all times, especially in natural bodies of water.

As you embark on summer water adventures, ensure your family's safety by following a few essential tips. Enroll your children in swimming lessons to develop their water skills and confidence. Teach them about water safety, including the importance of wearing life jackets when necessary and staying within designated swimming areas. Always supervise children closely around water and be vigilant of potential hazards.

So, dear adventurers, embrace the seasons and dive into the joys of winter sports and summer water fun with your school-age children. From exhilarating ski slopes to thrilling water slides, these seasonal adventures provide endless opportunities for laughter, bonding, and creating memories that will last a lifetime. Whether you're conquering the slopes or making a splash, let the seasons guide your family's journey into the colorful world of seasonal adventures!

Preserving Nature's Treasures: Inspiring Environmental Stewards!

As we embark on family adventures, let's not forget the profound impact we can have on the world around us. In this section, we'll delve into the importance of nature conservation and environmental awareness when traveling with school-age children. We'll discuss ways to teach children about the significance of preserving nature, share eco-friendly practices for sustainable travel, and recommend organizations and resources for further learning. Together, we can inspire the next generation of environmental stewards!

Teaching Children about the Importance of Nature Conservation:
Imagine your children's eyes widening in wonder as they explore the beauty of nature. It is within these precious moments that we have the opportunity to foster a deep connection and sense of responsibility towards the environment. Engage your children in conversations about the importance of preserving nature's treasures. Discuss the impact of human actions on ecosystems and the role each individual can play in conservation efforts. By instilling a sense of stewardship, we empower children to become champions for the environment.

Engaging in Eco-Friendly Practices while Traveling:
As we venture to new destinations, let's embark on eco-friendly journeys that leave a positive footprint on our planet. Encourage your children to embrace sustainable practices while traveling. Start with simple actions, like carrying reusable water bottles and shopping bags to reduce plastic waste. Opt for eco-friendly accommodations that prioritize energy efficiency and waste management. Respect wildlife and natural habitats, refraining from feeding or disturbing animals. Explore public transportation or opt for biking and walking whenever possible. By making conscious choices, we teach our children the importance of minimizing our impact on the environment.

Recommending Organizations and Resources for Further Learning:

To nurture a deeper understanding of nature conservation and environmental awareness, there are various organizations and resources that offer educational opportunities for families. Consider visiting nature centers, botanical gardens, or wildlife rehabilitation centers that provide hands-on learning experiences. National parks and nature reserves often offer ranger-led programs and Junior Ranger activities designed to educate and engage children in environmental conservation. Online platforms and books dedicated to environmental education, such as National Geographic Kids and The Lorax by Dr. Seuss, can spark curiosity and provide valuable insights into the importance of preserving our planet.

Additionally, supporting reputable organizations committed to conservation efforts can make a significant impact. Consider donating to or volunteering with organizations like the World Wildlife Fund, National Audubon Society, or local conservation groups. Engage with their resources, workshops, and campaigns that promote environmental awareness. By involving your children in these initiatives, they can witness firsthand the positive change that can be achieved through collective action.

Remember, dear adventurers, our planet is a precious gift, and we have the power to protect and preserve it for future generations. Through teaching children about nature conservation, practicing eco-friendly habits, and engaging with organizations and resources, we inspire a lifelong love and respect for the environment. Together, let's nurture a generation of environmental stewards who will champion the cause of preserving nature's wonders and ensuring a vibrant and sustainable future for all.

Chapter 8

Educational Excursions - Learning Beyond the Classroom

The Palmer family embarked on an educational and adventure-packed journey to Washington, D.C., with a mission to explore the world-renowned Smithsonian museums. With four kids in tow—Kate, Jaxon, Ava, and Liam—they were prepared for a day of curiosity, discovery, and, of course, a touch of mischief.

Their first stop was the National Air and Space Museum, a paradise for young minds fascinated by the wonders of flight and space exploration. As they entered the museum, their eyes widened at the sight of life-sized rockets and intricate aircraft suspended from the ceiling.

Jaxon, the family's resident science enthusiast, couldn't contain his excitement and darted off towards the space exhibit, eager to learn everything about the cosmos. The rest of the family followed closely, prepared for an intergalactic adventure.

As they explored the exhibits, the Palmer kids eagerly absorbed the fascinating information presented. They marveled at moon rocks, took turns sitting in astronaut simulators, and admired the spacesuits worn by real-life space explorers.

But amidst the awe-inspiring displays, a mischievous streak surfaced. Liam, the youngest of the bunch, discovered a button labeled "Press for Launch Experience" next to a mock rocket ship. Unable to resist, he pressed it, expecting nothing more than lights and sound effects.

To his surprise—and the Palmer family's amusement—the rocket ship began to shake, lights flashed, and the room filled with booming sound effects, mimicking the exhilaration of a real rocket launch. Liam's eyes widened, and he turned to his siblings with a mix of awe and panic.

The entire exhibit watched in amusement as the Palmer kids laughed and shouted, caught up in the unexpected thrill of the impromptu rocket launch. Their infectious laughter and wide smiles spread throughout the room, turning the exhibit into a joyful celebration of imagination and discovery.

Amidst the chaos, a museum staff member approached the Palmer family, chuckling at the scene. Instead of scolding them, she joined in on the laughter and shared her own anecdotes of mischievous moments she had witnessed in the museum.

The Palmer family continued their exploration of the Smithsonian museums, moving from one exhibit to another, their laughter and sense of adventure never faltering. Each museum offered a unique experience, and they reveled in the opportunity to expand their knowledge and create lifelong memories together.

As they left the Smithsonian museums, the Palmer family carried with them a newfound appreciation for the power of learning and the joy that comes from embracing the unexpected. They walked away with more than just facts and figures—they gained a deeper connection as a family, strengthened by the shared experiences and laughter they had found within the walls of the museums.

Welcome to the vibrant world of educational excursions, where learning extends far beyond the confines of a classroom! As a lifelong educator, I am thrilled to share with you the secret to turning your family vacation into a thrilling and enlightening journey. Prepare to embark on an adventure that combines the excitement of exploration with the joy of discovery, captivating the minds of your school-age children in ways they never imagined.

In this section, we will unearth destinations and activities that transform ordinary family vacations into extraordinary educational opportunities. Buckle up and get ready to immerse yourselves in a world where history comes alive, science becomes an adventure, and cultures unfold before your very eyes.

Gone are the days of mundane field trips and tedious lectures. We will guide you through the realm of educational exploration, where curiosity is celebrated, questions are encouraged, and the quest for knowledge is met with boundless enthusiasm. Get ready to witness the spark of inspiration ignite within your children's hearts as they uncover new worlds and broaden their horizons.

Together, we will delve into the treasure trove of destinations with educational value, ranging from awe-inspiring historical sites to interactive science centers that will leave your little scientists wide-eyed with wonder. We'll traverse the paths of ancient civilizations, unravel the mysteries of the natural world, and immerse ourselves in diverse cultures, fostering a deep appreciation for the tapestry of humanity.

But it's not all about facts and figures. We'll show you how to infuse fun into learning, striking a harmonious balance between education and entertainment. Picture your children's faces lighting up as they participate in hands-on experiments, engage in interactive exhibits, and embark on thrilling adventures through breathtaking landscapes.

As we journey together, we'll also explore the importance of cultural immersion, language learning, and the tantalizing world of local cuisine. Your family will have the chance to embrace new customs, sample mouthwatering delicacies, and communicate in different languages, enriching their understanding of the world and fostering a global mindset.

Throughout this section, we'll share invaluable tips and insights from a seasoned educator's perspective, helping you maximize the educational value of every moment. From sparking meaningful discussions to encouraging your children to keep travel journals or explore educational apps, we'll empower you to create a truly immersive and transformative experience.

So, fellow adventurers, join me on this exhilarating journey of educational excursions. Let's inspire a lifelong love for exploration, nurture insatiable curiosity, and embark on an extraordinary travel experience that will forever shape the minds and hearts of your school-age children. The world is waiting, and the possibilities for learning beyond the classroom are endless!

Preparing for Educational Excursions - Unveiling the Path to Enrichment!

Are you ready to embark on an educational adventure that will ignite the flames of curiosity within your school-age children? Before we set off on this thrilling journey, let's dive into the art of preparation. Like an artist with a palette, we will skillfully research and plan, ensuring that every moment of your educational excursion bursts with vibrancy and wonder.

Researching destinations with educational value: Unveiling Treasures

Imagine stepping foot in a land where history echoes through ancient walls, where science unveils its mesmerizing secrets, and where nature's wonders unfold in all their majesty. This is the world of educational destinations, waiting to be discovered by eager minds. Let's dig in!

Historical sites and landmarks: Unearthing the Past

Prepare to be transported back in time as you explore historical sites and landmarks. Wander through the corridors of centuries-old castles, stand in awe beneath iconic monuments, and trace the footsteps of legendary figures. Whether it's the Great Wall of China, the Colosseum in Rome, or the Pyramids of Giza, each step will immerse your family in the rich tapestry of human history.

Museums and science centers: Curiosity's Playground

Museums and science centers are like portals to another dimension, where learning takes center stage in the most captivating way. Unleash the inquisitive spirit within your children as they engage with interactive exhibits, marvel at ancient artifacts, and unravel the mysteries of the universe. From the Louvre in Paris to the Smithsonian Institution in Washington, D.C., prepare for an extraordinary voyage of discovery.

Nature reserves and national parks: Embracing the Great Outdoors

Nature's classroom awaits! Lace up your hiking boots, grab your binoculars, and venture into the breathtaking landscapes of nature reserves and national parks. Traverse winding trails, breathe in the crisp air, and witness the marvels of flora and fauna. From the vast Serengeti in Tanzania to the magnificent Yellowstone National Park in the United States, these natural wonders will captivate and inspire your family's love for the environment.

Planning age-appropriate activities: Crafting the Perfect Experience

Now that we've unearthed a treasure trove of destinations, it's time to tailor your educational excursion to the unique interests and passions of your school-age children. Let's create a symphony of experiences that harmonize learning and entertainment, ensuring that every moment leaves them wide-eyed and eager for more.

Tailoring activities to children's interests: Fueling the Flame of Curiosity

Every child has a world of interests waiting to be explored. Whether they're fascinated by dinosaurs, space exploration, or art, consider destinations and activities that align with their passions. Imagine their faces lighting up as they come face-to-face with a T-Rex skeleton at a natural history museum or create their own masterpiece at an art workshop. When learning aligns with their interests, the journey becomes even more captivating.

Considering interactive exhibits and hands-on experiences: Learning in Action

Let's break free from the confines of traditional learning and embrace the magic of interactivity. Seek out destinations that offer hands-on experiences, where your children can touch, experiment, and engage with the subject matter. From science experiments at interactive science centers to archaeological digs at historical sites, these immersive encounters will leave a lasting impression and deepen their understanding of the world around them.

Balancing educational content with entertainment: The Art of Edutainment

Education should never be a dull affair. Strike a harmonious balance between enriching educational content and captivating entertainment. Seek out destinations and activities that infuse learning with joy and excitement. Imagine your children's laughter as they participate in a historical reenactment or their awe as they witness a spectacular science show. By blending education and entertainment seamlessly, you'll create memories that will be cherished for a lifetime.

As you prepare for your educational excursion, remember that each step you take in the planning process adds color and depth to your journey. Through thorough research and thoughtful planning, you'll unlock a world of wonders and create a tapestry of experiences that will captivate your school-age children. Get ready to embark on an adventure like no other, where education and exploration intertwine to create a masterpiece of lifelong learning!

Cultural Immersion and Language Learning - Embrace the Tapestry of Humanity!

Prepare to embark on a captivating journey where cultures come alive, traditions unfold, and languages weave tales of their own. In this section, we will delve into the vibrant realm of cultural immersion and language learning, unlocking the doors to a world of understanding, connection, and global exploration.

Exploring different cultures and traditions: A Kaleidoscope of Diversity

Imagine stepping foot into a tapestry of cultures, each one boasting its own unique traditions, customs, and celebrations. From the bustling streets of Tokyo to the colorful markets of Marrakech, every corner of the world holds a treasure trove of cultural experiences waiting to be discovered. Immerse yourselves in local festivals, witness traditional dances, savor regional delicacies, and let the spirit of different cultures ignite your senses. Through these encounters, your family will develop a deep appreciation for the richness and diversity of our global family.

Engaging in local customs and traditions: Dancing to the Rhythm of Local Life

Break free from the role of an observer and become an active participant in the tapestry of local customs and traditions. Embrace the warmth of a traditional greeting, learn the art of tea ceremonies, or join in the spirited beats of a local dance. By embracing these customs, you and your children will forge meaningful connections with the communities you visit, fostering a sense of unity and mutual respect.

Learning basic phrases and practicing foreign languages: Unlocking the Power of Communication

Language is the key that unlocks the hearts and minds of people around the world. Encourage your children to venture beyond their linguistic comfort zones by learning basic phrases and practicing foreign languages. Mastering simple greetings, expressing gratitude, and engaging in basic conversations will not only enhance their travel experiences but also cultivate empathy and understanding. From "Bonjour" in Paris to "Kon'nichiwa" in Tokyo, these linguistic bridges will create lasting connections and open doors to authentic cultural exchanges.

Participating in cultural workshops or classes: Becoming a Cultural Connoisseur

Take your cultural immersion to the next level by participating in engaging workshops or classes. Whether it's learning traditional arts and crafts, trying your hand at local culinary delights, or mastering traditional music and dance, these hands-on experiences will allow your family to delve deep into the essence of a culture. Channel your inner artist, unleash your culinary creativity, or sway to the rhythms of ancient melodies. Through these interactive encounters, you will gain a profound appreciation for the intricate layers that shape a culture's identity.

As you embrace cultural immersion and language learning, remember that you are embarking on a transformative journey that transcends borders. Each encounter with a different culture and language is an opportunity to broaden your perspective, nurture empathy, and celebrate the beautiful tapestry of humanity. From engaging in local customs to communicating in a foreign tongue, these experiences will leave an indelible mark on your family's hearts and minds. Get ready to dance, taste, speak, and create your way through a world of diverse cultures, forging connections that will last a lifetime!

STEM-Based Adventures - Unleash the Power of Curiosity!

Calling all young explorers, budding scientists, and future inventors! Get ready to embark on a thrilling journey into the world of STEM-based adventures. In this section, we will unlock the secrets of science, technology, engineering, and mathematics, as we delve into a realm where wonder and innovation collide.

Visiting science museums and planetariums: A Universe of Discovery

Prepare to be dazzled by the wonders of the cosmos and the marvels of scientific exploration. Step into the realm of science museums and planetariums, where the mysteries of the universe await. From interactive exhibits that reveal the inner workings of the human body to planetarium shows that transport you to distant galaxies, these captivating spaces will ignite your children's curiosity and spark their fascination with the world of science.

Exploring technology and innovation centers: Where Imagination Takes Flight

Enter the realm where innovation and technology converge, inspiring minds and pushing the boundaries of what is possible. Explore technology and innovation centers that showcase cutting-edge advancements and inventions. From robotics labs where your children can build their own machines to virtual reality experiences that transport them to new dimensions, these futuristic spaces will leave them wide-eyed with awe and inspire their own creative thinking.

Engaging in hands-on experiments and demonstrations: Igniting the Spark of Discovery

Let your children's inner scientists take center stage as they engage in hands-on experiments and demonstrations. Encourage them to roll up their sleeves, put on their safety goggles, and immerse themselves in the world of discovery. From chemistry experiments that create colorful reactions to physics demonstrations that defy gravity, these engaging activities will foster a love for learning by allowing them to experience science in action.

Discovering natural wonders and ecological sites: Nature's Laboratory

Venture beyond the confines of a laboratory and step into nature's own classroom. Discover the wonders of ecological sites and natural landscapes that hold the secrets to our planet's biodiversity. Whether it's exploring coral reefs teeming with marine life, hiking through lush rainforests, or observing wildlife in their natural habitats, these encounters with the natural world will instill a sense of wonder and foster a deep appreciation for the importance of ecological preservation.

Top ten STEM related vacation spots for you and your kiddos:

1. Kennedy Space Center, Florida, USA: Located on the east coast of Florida, the Kennedy Space Center is NASA's primary launch site. Families can explore interactive exhibits, tour space shuttle launch pads, and even meet real astronauts. It's a great place to learn about space exploration and the history of space travel.

2. Smithsonian National Air and Space Museum, Washington, D.C., USA: Situated in the heart of the US capital, the Smithsonian National

Air and Space Museum offers a vast collection of aircraft, spacecraft, and other artifacts. Kids can see the Wright Brothers' plane, lunar modules, and the iconic Apollo 11 command module. The museum also hosts interactive displays and educational programs.

3. Exploratorium, San Francisco, California, USA: The Exploratorium is a hands-on science museum that encourages visitors to explore the world through interactive exhibits. With hundreds of exhibits covering a wide range of scientific disciplines, it's an ideal place for kids to learn about physics, biology, and other STEM subjects in a fun and engaging way.

4. CERN, Geneva, Switzerland: CERN (European Organization for Nuclear Research) is one of the world's leading centers for particle physics. Families can take guided tours to see the Large Hadron Collider (LHC) and learn about cutting-edge research in the field of particle physics. It's a fantastic opportunity to understand the fundamental building blocks of the universe.

5. Epcot, Florida, USA: Part of the Walt Disney World Resort, Epcot features Future World, a section dedicated to innovation and technology. Kids can explore interactive exhibits on topics like energy, communication, and space travel. The World Showcase also offers a glimpse into different cultures and their contributions to science and technology.

6. Smithsonian National Museum of Natural History, Washington, D.C., USA: The Smithsonian National Museum of Natural History is home to an incredible collection of natural history exhibits. Kids can discover dinosaur fossils, gemstones, and learn about ecosystems and biodiversity. The museum also features interactive displays on human evolution and the natural world.

7. The Tech Interactive, San Jose, California, USA: The Tech Interactive is an interactive science and technology museum that encourages visitors to engage with hands-on exhibits. Kids can explore robotics, virtual reality, and learn about innovations in various fields. The museum also hosts workshops and demonstrations to foster curiosity and creativity.

8. Natural History Museum, London, UK: The Natural History Museum in London is renowned for its extensive collection of specimens and artifacts. Kids can see dinosaur skeletons, fossils, and learn about natural phenomena like earthquakes and volcanoes. The museum's interactive exhibits offer a captivating exploration of Earth's history and biodiversity.

9. Ontario Science Centre, Toronto, Canada: The Ontario Science Centre provides a wide range of exhibits and activities for families. Kids can experiment with physics, biology, and chemistry in the hands-on Discovery Zone. The center also features an IMAX theater and planetarium, offering immersive educational experiences.

10. Space Center Houston, Texas, USA: Space Center Houston is the official visitor center for NASA's Johnson Space Center. Families can take guided tram tours, explore the extensive exhibits on space exploration, and even touch moon rocks. The center also offers interactive shows and presentations by astronauts, inspiring the next generation of space enthusiasts.

As you embark on these STEM-based adventures, remember that you are nurturing the innovators and problem solvers of tomorrow. Each visit to a science museum, every hands-on experiment, and each encounter with the wonders of nature will fuel your children's curiosity and ignite their passion for STEM subjects. Encourage them to ask questions, to explore, and to dream big. The world of science and innovation is waiting to be discovered, and your family is poised to make remarkable discoveries along the way. So, get ready to unlock the secrets of the universe, to create and innovate, and to embark on an adventure that will shape the future of your young scientists. Let the magic of STEM-based adventures guide you on an extraordinary journey of exploration and discovery!

Historical and Archaeological Explorations - Unveiling the Tapestry of the Past!

Step back in time and embark on a captivating journey through the annals of history. In this section, we invite you to uncover the secrets of ancient civilizations, walk in the footsteps of legendary figures, and immerse yourselves in the rich tapestry of human heritage. Get ready to ignite the flames of curiosity and explore the wonders of historical and archaeological sites!

Exploring ancient ruins and historical sites: Timeless Treasures

Picture yourself standing amidst ancient ruins, where the whispers of the past echo through the stones. Explore majestic pyramids, wander through crumbling castles, or meander along cobblestone streets that have witnessed centuries of human history. As you immerse yourselves in these hallowed grounds, let your imaginations soar, and let the stories of bygone eras come alive. From the mystical Machu Picchu in Peru to the awe-inspiring Acropolis in Greece, each historical site holds a treasure trove of wonders waiting to be discovered.

Visiting living history museums and reenactments: Stepping into the Past

Step beyond the pages of history books and find yourself immersed in living history museums and reenactments. Witness the past come alive as costumed interpreters recreate historic events, bringing the stories of yesteryear to life. Participate in interactive demonstrations, try on period costumes, and engage in activities that transport you back in time. Whether it's a colonial village in Williamsburg, USA, or a medieval fair in Europe, these experiences will ignite your children's imagination and provide a deeper understanding of historical contexts.

Participating in guided tours and educational programs: A Guided Journey

Let knowledgeable guides lead the way as you unravel the layers of history through guided tours and educational programs. Engage with passionate experts who will share fascinating stories and insights, shedding light on the significance of each site. Whether it's a captivating walking tour through ancient ruins or a specialized workshop on archaeological techniques, these educational experiences will deepen your appreciation for the intricacies of the past and foster a love for history.

Learning about local history and heritage: The Soul of a Place

Every destination has a unique story to tell, woven with threads of local history and heritage. Take the time to learn about the communities you visit, their customs, and their rich cultural legacies. Visit local museums, explore heritage sites, and engage with locals who carry the torch of tradition. By understanding the local history and heritage, you will gain a profound appreciation for the people and the places that make each destination so extraordinary.

Here's a list of the top ten history and archaeological-related vacation spots in the US and around the world, along with descriptions of each destination. These places offer immersive experiences that bring history and archaeology to life, making them ideal for families with school-age children.

1. The Pyramids of Giza, Egypt: The Pyramids of Giza are a UNESCO World Heritage site and one of the Seven Wonders of the Ancient World. Families can explore the Great Pyramid of Khufu, the Sphinx, and nearby archaeological sites. It's an opportunity to marvel at the engineering feats of the ancient Egyptians and learn about their civilization.

2. Pompeii, Italy: The ancient city of Pompeii, near Naples, offers a fascinating glimpse into Roman life before the catastrophic eruption of Mount Vesuvius in 79 AD. Families can wander through remarkably preserved streets, visit ancient homes, and see the haunting plaster casts of volcanic victims. It's an immersive archaeological experience.

3. Machu Picchu, Peru: Machu Picchu is an ancient Incan city perched high in the Andes Mountains. Families can explore the well-preserved ruins, hike the Inca Trail, and learn about the sophisticated engineering and agricultural practices of the Incas. The breathtaking scenery adds to the allure of this UNESCO World Heritage site.

4. Colonial Williamsburg, Virginia, USA: Colonial Williamsburg is a living history museum where families can step back in time to the 18th century. Costumed interpreters bring the colonial period to life, showcasing trades, politics, and everyday life. Visitors can explore historic buildings, participate in interactive activities, and gain insights into American history.

5. Acropolis of Athens, Greece: The Acropolis, located in Athens, is an ancient citadel atop a hill. Families can marvel at the Parthenon, the Erechtheion, and other ancient structures that represent the pinnacle of classical Greek architecture. Guided tours and multimedia exhibits provide historical context and highlight the cultural significance of this iconic site.

6. Mesa Verde National Park, Colorado, USA: Mesa Verde National Park is home to some of the best-preserved Native American cliff dwellings in North America. Families can explore these ancient Puebloan ruins, learn about the lives of the Ancestral Puebloans, and discover their unique architecture and culture. The park offers guided tours and educational programs for all ages.

7. The Colosseum, Rome, Italy: The Colosseum is an iconic symbol of ancient Rome and a UNESCO World Heritage site. Families can tour this immense amphitheater, learn about gladiatorial contests, and understand the grandeur of ancient spectacles. Interactive displays and guided tours shed light on the fascinating history of the Colosseum and its significance.

8. Chichen Itza, Mexico: Chichen Itza is a Mayan archaeological site on the Yucatan Peninsula. Families can explore the towering El Castillo pyramid, the Temple of Warriors, and the Great Ball Court. The site's rich history and architectural marvels provide an immersive experience that allows visitors to appreciate the ancient Mayan civilization.

9. Independence National Historical Park, Pennsylvania, USA: Independence National Historical Park in Philadelphia is home to the Liberty Bell and Independence Hall, where the Declaration of Independence and the US Constitution were signed. Families can visit these historic landmarks, explore museums, and engage in interactive exhibits that delve into the birth of the United States.

10. Stonehenge, England, UK: Stonehenge is an enigmatic prehistoric monument located in Wiltshire. Families can marvel at the towering stone megaliths, learn about the theories surrounding its purpose and construction, and explore the nearby visitor center. Audio guides and interactive displays provide insights into the ancient cultures that built Stonehenge.

These history and archaeological-related vacation spots offer a blend of education and exploration, providing families with unforgettable experiences that connect them with the rich tapestry of human history.

As you embark on these historical and archaeological explorations, remember that you are treading upon the foundations of human civilization. Each step you take will bring you closer to understanding the triumphs, struggles, and innovations of those who came before us. Let the mysteries of the past capture your family's imagination, and let the stories engraved in ancient stones ignite a passion for history within your school-age children. Get ready to travel through time, to walk hand in hand with history, and to create memories that will be cherished for generations to come. So, don your explorer's hat, grab your map, and embark on an extraordinary journey through the corridors of time!

Nature and Environmental Education - Embrace the Wonders of the Natural World!

Get ready to embark on an extraordinary adventure into the arms of Mother Nature herself. In this section, we invite you and your family to immerse yourselves in the breathtaking beauty of the great outdoors. It's time to connect with the natural world, learn about its wonders, and become stewards of our precious planet. Let's dive into the realm of nature and environmental education!

Exploring national parks and wildlife reserves: Nature's Masterpieces

Enter a world where towering trees, majestic mountains, and shimmering lakes paint a mesmerizing backdrop. National parks and wildlife reserves are nature's masterpieces, waiting to be explored. Roam the trails, breathe in the crisp air, and marvel at the diversity of flora and fauna that call these protected lands home. From the untamed beauty of the Amazon Rainforest to the awe-inspiring landscapes of

Yellowstone National Park, every step will bring you closer to the wonders of our natural heritage.

Participating in guided nature walks and hikes: Trails of Discovery

Tie up your shoelaces, grab your backpacks, and join expert guides on exhilarating nature walks and hikes. Traverse winding trails, where every turn reveals a new marvel of the natural world. Learn to identify different plant species, listen to the harmonies of bird songs, and spot elusive wildlife hiding amidst the foliage. With each step, you and your children will deepen your connection to nature and develop a profound respect for its delicate balance.

Learning about biodiversity and conservation efforts: Guardians of the Earth

Uncover the intricate web of life and learn about the importance of biodiversity and conservation efforts. Engage with experts who are dedicated to preserving our planet's natural wonders. Through informative sessions and interactive exhibits, discover the delicate balance of ecosystems, understand the threats they face, and explore the innovative solutions being implemented to protect them. From marine conservation centers to educational exhibits on deforestation, these experiences will empower your family to become passionate stewards of the Earth.

Engaging in eco-friendly practices and sustainability initiatives: Agents of Change

Step into the role of eco-conscious travelers by engaging in eco-friendly practices and embracing sustainability initiatives. Learn about responsible tourism and how your actions can make a positive impact on the environment. Whether it's participating in beach clean-ups, supporting local conservation projects, or choosing eco-friendly accommodations, your choices as a family can contribute to the preservation of our planet's natural treasures. By practicing sustainable habits, you'll inspire your children to become lifelong advocates for a greener, more sustainable world.

Here are ten of the most educational nature destinations from around the US and the world that I recommend visiting with your school age kids:

1. Yellowstone National Park, Wyoming, USA: Yellowstone National Park is the world's first national park and a UNESCO World Heritage site. Families can explore its geothermal wonders, including the iconic Old Faithful geyser, colorful hot springs, and bubbling mud pots. The park is also home to diverse wildlife, such as bison, bears, and wolves, providing endless opportunities for educational experiences in a breathtaking natural setting.

2. Galapagos Islands, Ecuador: The Galapagos Islands are a remote archipelago in the Pacific Ocean known for their incredible biodiversity and unique wildlife. Families can observe giant tortoises, marine iguanas, and blue-footed boobies up close. The islands offer educational tours and guided activities, allowing children to learn about the fragile ecosystems and ongoing conservation efforts.

3. Great Barrier Reef, Australia: The Great Barrier Reef is the world's largest coral reef system, stretching over 2,300 kilometers (1,400 miles) along the coast of Queensland. Families can embark on snorkeling or diving adventures to witness the vibrant marine life, including coral formations and a plethora of fish species. Educational programs teach about the importance of reef conservation and the impacts of climate change.

4. Denali National Park, Alaska, USA: Denali National Park is home to North America's tallest peak, Denali (formerly Mount McKinley). Families

can explore the park's vast wilderness, spot wildlife like grizzly bears and moose, and take part in ranger-led programs focused on nature, ecology, and conservation. The park's dramatic landscapes provide an excellent backdrop for learning about Alaska's natural heritage.

5. Amazon Rainforest, Brazil: The Amazon Rainforest is the world's largest tropical rainforest, known for its incredible biodiversity and ecological significance. Families can embark on guided tours to observe diverse plant and animal species, learn about indigenous cultures, and gain insights into rainforest conservation efforts. It's an opportunity to understand the importance of preserving this vital ecosystem.

6. Rocky Mountain National Park, Colorado, USA: Rocky Mountain National Park offers a breathtaking alpine experience with soaring peaks, lush valleys, and abundant wildlife. Families can explore the park's scenic trails, participate in educational programs, and attend ranger-led talks that delve into topics like geology, ecology, and animal adaptations. The park's diverse ecosystems provide a rich learning environment.

7. Borneo, Malaysia: Borneo is a tropical paradise known for its lush rainforests, diverse wildlife, and unique plant species. Families can take guided tours through the rainforest, spot orangutans in their natural habitat, and learn about conservation efforts to protect endangered species. Borneo offers an immersive experience in one of the world's most biologically diverse regions.

8. Everglades National Park, Florida, USA: Everglades National Park is a unique wetland ecosystem that is home to rare and endangered species. Families can explore the park's vast network of mangroves, sawgrass marshes, and cypress swamps through boat tours or guided hikes. Educational programs focus on topics like water conservation, ecosystem dynamics, and the importance of wetland preservation.

9. Costa Rica: Costa Rica is a small Central American country renowned for its biodiversity and commitment to environmental conservation. Families can visit national parks, hike through cloud forests, and encounter wildlife such as sloths, monkeys, and colorful birds. Eco-lodges and nature reserves offer educational programs that teach about sustainable practices and wildlife protection.

10. Serengeti National Park, Tanzania: Serengeti National Park is a world-famous wildlife sanctuary known for the annual wildebeest migration. Families can witness this incredible natural spectacle and observe diverse wildlife, including lions, elephants, and giraffes. Guided safaris provide opportunities for educational experiences focused on animal behavior, conservation, and the importance of preserving Africa's iconic savannah ecosystems.

These nature and environmental education-related vacation spots offer families the chance to immerse themselves in the wonders of the natural world. They provide educational programs, guided tours, and interactive experiences that promote environmental awareness and foster a deep appreciation for the Earth's ecosystems.

As you dive into the realm of nature and environmental education, remember that you are embarking on a transformative journey that extends far beyond the beauty of the landscapes. Each encounter with the natural world will open your eyes to its wonders, teaching you and your children the importance of conservation and our role as caretakers of the Earth. So, take a deep breath, listen to the whispers of the wind, and let the vibrant colors of nature ignite your spirits. Get ready to explore, learn, and protect the incredible wonders of our planet. Together, we can make a difference and create a future where nature thrives in all its magnificence!

Tips for Maximizing Educational Value - Unleashing the Power of Learning!

As you embark on your family adventure, let's unlock the secrets to maximizing the educational value of every moment. In this section, we'll dive into a treasure trove of tips and strategies that will transform your journey into a captivating and enriching experience. Get ready to infuse every step of your trip with learning, curiosity, and discovery!

Incorporating educational discussions during the trip: Conversations that Spark Knowledge

Take advantage of the natural wonders and cultural encounters that unfold before you by incorporating educational discussions into your family's journey. Engage your children in conversations about the history, geography, and unique features of each destination. Ask thought-provoking questions and encourage them to share their observations and reflections. From pondering the engineering marvels of ancient civilizations to discussing the environmental impact of our actions, these conversations will ignite their curiosity and foster a deeper understanding of the world around them.

Keeping a travel journal or scrapbook: Capturing Memories and Insights

Transform your children into budding explorers and storytellers by encouraging them to keep a travel journal or create a scrapbook. Provide them with blank pages or a camera to document their experiences, allowing them to record their observations, sketch their surroundings, and jot down fascinating facts they've learned. By capturing memories and insights, they'll create a tangible keepsake that reflects their unique perspective and the knowledge they've gained during the journey.

Utilizing educational apps and online resources: Learning at Your Fingertips

In this digital age, educational apps and online resources can be invaluable tools to enhance your family's learning experience. Discover interactive apps that provide engaging content about the destinations you visit, offer language-learning opportunities, or teach scientific concepts through fun games. Tap into online resources that provide historical information, virtual tours, or educational videos that complement your travel experiences. With technology as your guide, you'll unlock a world of knowledge and interactive learning right at your fingertips.

Encouraging children to ask questions and be curious: Fueling the Flame of Wonder

Nurture the natural curiosity within your children by encouraging them to ask questions and explore their surroundings with wide-eyed wonder. Create a safe and supportive environment where no question is too small or insignificant. Encourage them to inquire about the cultures, environments, and phenomena they encounter. By embracing their curiosity, you'll empower them to become lifelong learners, forever seeking answers and uncovering the marvels of the world.

As you incorporate these tips into your family's travel experience, remember that learning knows no bounds. Each moment of your journey holds the potential for discovery, connection, and personal growth. So, engage in educational discussions, capture memories in journals, embrace the power of technology, and encourage the insatiable curiosity within your children. Let the joy of learning be a constant companion as you explore the world together. Through these simple yet powerful strategies, you'll create an extraordinary adventure that will shape their minds and hearts, forever fueling their thirst for knowledge. The world is your classroom, and the journey of learning is infinite!

Embrace the Journey of Learning and Discovery!

As we reach the end of this section, let's take a moment to reflect on the incredible benefits of educational excursions and the transformative power they hold. We have witnessed the spark of curiosity igniting within your children, the joy of exploration fueling their hearts, and the thirst for knowledge propelling them forward. This is just the beginning of a lifelong journey of learning and discovery!

Unleashing the Potential

Educational excursions have the power to unlock hidden potentials within your children. They transcend traditional learning environments, opening doors to immersive experiences and hands-on discoveries. Through historical explorations, STEM-based adventures, cultural immersion, and nature education, your children have had the opportunity to broaden their horizons, deepen their understanding, and foster a sense of global citizenship. These excursions have nurtured their curiosity, ignited their passion for learning, and sparked a desire to make a positive impact on the world around them.

Creating Lasting Connections

As you embark on these educational excursions, remember that learning is not limited to your children alone. Embrace the journey as a family, experiencing the wonder and joy of discovery side by side. Engage in conversations that inspire, ask questions that challenge, and learn from one another. By exploring and learning together, you create lasting connections, strengthening the bond within your family and creating cherished memories that will be treasured for a lifetime.

Unleash the Adventurer Within

The adventures you embark on today will shape the future of your children. Through educational excursions, you are instilling a lifelong love for travel and education, nurturing their inquisitive spirits, and empowering them to become lifelong learners and explorers of the world. The experiences they have had and the knowledge they have gained will serve as stepping stones for their future endeavors, opening doors to new opportunities and shaping their perspectives on life.

So, fellow adventurers, as you continue your journey, let the fire of curiosity burn bright within you. Explore the world with wide-eyed wonder, seek knowledge with insatiable hunger, and embrace the transformative power of educational excursions. Together, let's create a world where learning knows no bounds, where the beauty of the world is celebrated, and where the journey of exploration never ends. Travel with open minds, embrace the joy of discovery, and inspire the love for travel and education in the hearts of your children. The world is waiting, and the adventure continues!

Chapter 9

Keeping Kids Engaged - Entertainment and Activities on the Go

The Brown family embarked on a whirlwind adventure across the pond to visit the vibrant city of London. With their cameras and guidebooks in hand, they were ready to soak up the rich history and iconic landmarks.

Their first stop was the famous Buckingham Palace. As they stood outside the majestic gates, Mr. Brown decided to impress his family with a little trivia. He confidently declared, "Did you know the Queen once invited a commoner like me for tea?"

Mrs. Brown rolled her eyes playfully and replied, "Oh really? And when was this tea party?"

Mr. Brown, caught off guard, quickly improvised, "Well, it was a long time ago, you see. I think I was just a wee lad, and she must have forgotten about it."

The kids, sensing their dad's playful exaggeration, burst into laughter, teasing him about his royal tea escapades for the rest of the trip.

As they continued their London exploration, the Brown family found themselves navigating the bustling Underground system. Determined to conquer the confusing maze of tunnels, they approached a ticket booth.

Little Sarah, the youngest of the bunch, mustered up her courage and asked the attendant, "Excuse me, sir. How do we get to Platform 9¾?"

The attendant, in the spirit of fun, winked at Sarah and pointed to a nearby wall, saying, "Just run straight into that wall, and you'll find it!"

Sarah's eyes widened with anticipation as she prepared for her magical journey to Hogwarts. With a mischievous grin, she turned to her family, ready to take the leap into the world of Harry Potter.

However, much to her surprise—and the amusement of her family—Sarah crashed headfirst into the solid wall, her feet comically kicking up in the air. Passersby couldn't help but laugh at the unexpected spectacle.

Unfazed by the mishap, Sarah jumped up with a sheepish smile, shrugging her shoulders as if to say, "I guess my Hogwarts letter will have to wait."

The Brown family roared with laughter, helping Sarah to her feet. They turned the incident into a running joke for the remainder of their London adventure, affectionately referring to Platform 9¾ as the "Elusive Platform."

As the days flew by, the Brown family immersed themselves in London's rich culture and iconic landmarks. They climbed aboard the iconic double-decker buses, took comical photos with the statuesque guards at the Tower of London, and attempted their best British accents during afternoon tea.

Their journey through London became a blend of awe-inspiring moments and hilarious mishaps. And while they may not have had a royal tea with the Queen or successfully found Platform 9¾, the memories they created and the laughter they shared brought them closer as a family, forever cherishing their unforgettable adventure in the lively city of London.

Traveling with school-age children can be a delightful adventure filled with unforgettable moments and shared experiences. However, as any parent knows, long flights, train rides, or car journeys can also present challenges, particularly when it comes to keeping kids entertained and engaged. That's why this chapter is dedicated to the art of keeping your children happily occupied during travel, ensuring that boredom doesn't dampen their spirits or make the journey feel endless.

Keeping kids entertained during travel is essential for both their well-being and the overall enjoyment of the trip. When children are engaged in entertaining activities, it helps alleviate restlessness, reduces stress levels, and minimizes the likelihood of tantrums or meltdowns. By providing a range of engaging options, you can create a positive travel experience for your children, fostering their enthusiasm and curiosity about the world around them.

Engaging activities during travel offer numerous benefits for children. First and foremost, they help pass the time in an enjoyable and meaningful way, making the journey more enjoyable for everyone involved. Engaging activities also stimulate children's creativity, imagination, and cognitive skills, allowing them to explore new ideas and perspectives. Furthermore, these activities can enhance their problem-solving abilities, promote social interaction, and strengthen family bonds through shared experiences.

In this chapter, we will present a wide range of entertainment options and activities that are sure to captivate your children's imaginations and keep them happily engaged while on the go. We will provide suggestions for both traditional and technology-based games, as well as interactive activities that encourage creativity and exploration. Additionally, we will explore ways to engage with the surroundings, including nature-based and cultural activities that can enhance the travel experience for the whole family.

Moreover, we will discuss the importance of preparing for the journey by packing essential entertainment items and providing practical tips to ensure a smooth and enjoyable travel experience. From DIY travel activity kits and family-friendly podcasts to educational apps and outdoor adventures, this chapter aims to provide you with a plethora of options to cater to different interests and age groups.

By incorporating these engaging activities into your travel plans, you can transform your journey into a time of excitement, learning, and togetherness. So, let's dive in and discover the wonderful world of entertainment and activities on the go, ensuring that your family's travel memories are filled with joy and cherished moments that will last a lifetime.

Interactive Games and Activities

When it comes to keeping your kids entertained and engaged during travel, interactive games and activities are a fantastic way to capture their imaginations and make the journey more enjoyable. From traditional games that have stood the test of time to creative do-it-yourself kits and captivating audio experiences, there's something for everyone in this colorful world of entertainment.

Old fashioned fun (mostly)

Traditional games

1. I-Spy: A classic game that never gets old. Take turns choosing an object within sight and give clues by saying, "I spy with my little eye, something that is [color/shape/starts with a letter]." Encourage your children to use their observation skills and guess the object correctly.

2. 20 Questions: Challenge your kids' critical thinking skills with this game. Think of a person, place, or thing and let them ask up to 20 yes-or-no questions to guess what you're thinking. It's a great way to spark curiosity and promote deductive reasoning.

3. License plate game: Turn those boring license plates into a fun game. Have your children create words or phrases using the letters on passing license plates. See who can come up with the longest word or the most creative phrase.

Word games

1. Storytelling (collaborative or round-robin): Encourage your kids' imagination by creating a collaborative story. Each person takes turns adding a sentence or a paragraph to the ongoing tale. It's a delightful way to weave a unique narrative and engage everyone's creativity.

2. Rhyming games: Challenge your children to a rhyming contest. Take turns coming up with words that rhyme with a given word, and see who can come up with the most rhymes. It's a fantastic opportunity to enhance their vocabulary and have some lyrical fun.

3. Alphabet game (finding items starting with each letter): Start with the letter "A" and take turns finding objects or landmarks that begin with each subsequent letter of the alphabet. It's an interactive way to explore your surroundings and discover new things.

DIY travel activity kits

1. Craft kits (paper airplanes, friendship bracelets): Prepare a travel-friendly craft kit with materials for making paper airplanes or friendship bracelets. It's a hands-on activity that sparks creativity and keeps little hands busy during the journey.

2. Scavenger hunt game kits: Create a scavenger hunt game tailored to your travel destination. Make a list of specific items or landmarks your kids need to find, and let them embark on a thrilling adventure to check off each item on the list.

3. Magnetic puzzle kits: Magnetic puzzles are perfect for travel. These compact and reusable puzzles come in various themes and difficulty levels, keeping your children entertained and engaged as they solve puzzles on the go.

Family-friendly podcasts and audiobooks

1. Recommended podcasts for kids: Discover a wide range of entertaining and educational podcasts designed specifically for children. From adventure stories to science facts and everything in between, these podcasts are sure to captivate your kids' attention and spark their curiosity about the world.

Some of my favorite podcasts for a long journey with short attention spans:

1. "Wow in the World"
Description: Hosted by Guy Raz and Mindy Thomas, this podcast explores the wonders of science and technology through fun and engaging storytelling. Each episode takes listeners on a fascinating journey, unraveling mysteries and answering curious questions about the world around us.

2. "Brains On!"
Description: Join Molly Bloom and her team of kid hosts as they delve into intriguing topics like animals, space, and the human body. This educational podcast combines expert interviews, listener questions, and lively discussions to make learning an entertaining adventure.

3. "But Why: A Podcast for Curious Kids"
Description: In this podcast, host Jane Lindholm answers questions submitted by young listeners on a wide range of topics. From how robots work to why we dream, each episode provides curious minds with informative and engaging explanations.

4. "Story Pirates"
Description: Get ready for imaginative and hilarious stories brought to life by talented actors and comedians. "Story Pirates" features stories written by kids, inspiring creativity and encouraging young listeners to embrace their own storytelling abilities.

5. "The Alien Adventures of Finn Caspian"
Description: Follow Finn Caspian, a young boy aboard a spaceship, as he explores the galaxy and encounters strange creatures and interstellar mysteries. This serialized podcast offers a thrilling blend of adventure, humor, and science fiction.

6. "Smash Boom Best"
Description: Join host Molly Bloom as she pits two fascinating things against each other in friendly debates. From unicorns vs. dragons to chocolate vs. cheese, this podcast encourages critical thinking, research, and passionate discussion in a lighthearted and entertaining manner.

7. "Ear Snacks"
Description: Dive into the world of music, science, and creativity with "Ear Snacks." This delightful podcast features catchy songs, interesting interviews, and interactive games, stimulating curiosity and encouraging young minds to explore their own creative potentials.

8. "Stuff You Should Know"
Description: Hosts Josh and Chuck explore fascinating and often bizarre topics, providing in-depth explanations and fun facts about

everything from history and science to pop culture. "Stuff You Should Know" is an engaging podcast that offers endless learning opportunities for curious minds.

9. "The Radio Adventures of Dr. Floyd"
Description: Step into the world of time travel with Dr. Floyd and his companions, as they embark on comical adventures through history. This family-friendly podcast blends humor, educational tidbits, and lively characters, making it a perfect choice for entertaining road trips.

10. "Good Night Stories for Rebel Girls"
Description: Inspired by the bestselling book series, this podcast features extraordinary women from history and contemporary times. Each episode highlights the achievements and inspiring stories of remarkable women, encouraging empowerment, and fostering a sense of equality.

These podcasts provide captivating and educational content for the whole family, making vacation or road trips an opportunity for shared learning and meaningful discussions. So, load up your podcast app, press play, and embark on an audio adventure that will entertain, inform, and inspire both kids and adults alike.

Engaging audiobooks for family listening: Choose engaging audiobooks that the whole family can enjoy together. Whether it's a classic tale or a contemporary adventure, listening to audiobooks is a fantastic way to pass the time and create shared memories.

Here are a few recommendations of my favorite audiobooks for a family road trip with school age kids:

1. "Harry Potter" series by J.K. Rowling

Description: Join Harry, Ron, and Hermione on their magical adventures at Hogwarts School of Witchcraft and Wizardry. This beloved series, narrated by Jim Dale, is a fantastic choice for a family road trip, captivating listeners of all ages with its enchanting storytelling and memorable characters.

2. "The Chronicles of Narnia" series by C.S. Lewis
Description: Step through the wardrobe into the magical world of Narnia. This epic series, narrated by renowned actors like Michael York and Derek Jacobi, takes listeners on extraordinary adventures filled with talking animals, mythical creatures, and battles between good and evil.

3. "Matilda" by Roald Dahl
Description: Join Matilda, a brilliant and resourceful young girl, as she navigates her way through a world of unsympathetic adults and discovers her extraordinary abilities. Kate Winslet's captivating narration brings Roald Dahl's heartwarming and empowering tale to life.

4. "Percy Jackson & The Olympians" series by Rick Riordan
Description: Follow Percy Jackson, a demigod with incredible powers, as he embarks on thrilling quests and battles Greek mythology's most dangerous creatures. Jesse Bernstein's dynamic narration perfectly captures the humor and excitement of this action-packed series.

5. "The Secret Garden" by Frances Hodgson Burnett
Description: Enter the enchanting world of a hidden garden and witness the transformative power of nature. This timeless classic, narrated by various talented narrators, tells the story of a young girl's journey of self-discovery and the magic that blooms along the way.

6. "Charlotte's Web" by E.B. White
Description: Join Wilbur, the lovable pig, and Charlotte, the intelligent spider, on a heartwarming journey of friendship and courage. E.B.

White's tender tale, narrated by a cast of talented performers, explores themes of loyalty, empathy, and the beauty of the natural world.

7. "The Hobbit" by J.R.R. Tolkien
Description: Embark on a grand adventure with Bilbo Baggins as he accompanies a group of dwarves on a quest to reclaim their homeland. This epic fantasy, narrated by Rob Inglis, is filled with thrilling encounters, fantastical creatures, and a richly imagined world.

8. "Wonder" by R.J. Palacio
Description: Follow the inspiring story of Auggie Pullman, a young boy with facial differences, as he navigates the challenges of fitting in at a new school. This heartwarming tale, narrated by a talented cast, promotes empathy, kindness, and acceptance.

9. "The Lion, the Witch, and the Wardrobe" by C.S. Lewis
Description: Enter the magical land of Narnia through a wardrobe and witness the battle between the White Witch and Aslan the lion. Michael York's captivating narration brings this beloved tale of courage, sacrifice, and redemption to life.

10. "Alice's Adventures in Wonderland" by Lewis Carroll
Description: Join Alice on a whimsical journey down the rabbit hole into a world of peculiar characters and nonsensical situations. This imaginative classic, narrated by acclaimed performers, invites listeners to explore a topsy-turvy realm where anything is possible.

These captivating audiobooks are sure to make your family road trip an unforgettable experience, transporting you to magical worlds, inspiring you with courageous characters, and sparking meaningful discussions along the way. Buckle up, press play, and let the stories unfold!

Tips for creating a personalized travel playlist: Tailor a travel playlist that includes your kids' favorite songs, sing-alongs, and even some catchy travel-themed tunes. Music can evoke emotions and enhance the travel experience, making the journey feel more vibrant and exciting.

With these interactive games and activities at your disposal, the hours will fly by as your children dive into a world of imagination and entertainment. So pack your creativity, prepare for laughter, and embark on a journey filled with joyful moments and cherished memories. Let the games begin!

Technology-based Entertainment

In today's digital age, technology can be a valuable ally when it comes to keeping your kids entertained and engaged during travel. From educational apps and games that stimulate young minds to immersive virtual reality experiences, the possibilities for colorful and captivating entertainment are endless.

Educational apps and games

Language learning apps: Turn travel time into an opportunity for your children to learn a new language. Choose interactive language learning apps that make language acquisition fun and engaging. From vocabulary-building exercises to pronunciation practice, these apps offer an interactive way to explore different languages and cultures.

Here are a few of my favorite apps for immersing kids in the language of your destination prior to arrival:

1. Duolingo
Description: Duolingo is a popular and gamified language learning app that makes language acquisition fun and engaging for kids. With its interactive lessons, colorful visuals, and rewards system, Duolingo offers a variety of languages to learn, including Spanish, French,

German, and more. It covers vocabulary, pronunciation, and basic grammar, making it suitable for beginners.

2. Rosetta Stone Kids Lingo Letter Sounds
Description: Rosetta Stone Kids Lingo Letter Sounds is designed to introduce young children to the sounds and pronunciation of different languages. It focuses on letter sounds, vocabulary building, and early reading skills. The app utilizes engaging activities, stories, and songs to make language learning enjoyable for kids.

3. Memrise
Description: Memrise is an app that uses spaced repetition and mnemonic techniques to help kids memorize vocabulary effectively. It offers a wide range of language courses, including popular choices like Spanish, French, and Japanese. Memrise incorporates audio, video, and interactive exercises to engage learners of all ages.

4. Babbel
Description: Babbel is an app that offers interactive language courses for kids and adults. With its user-friendly interface and practical exercises, Babbel provides comprehensive lessons covering vocabulary, grammar, and conversation skills. It supports various languages, allowing kids to learn at their own pace and develop fluency over time.

5. Mindsnacks
Description: Mindsnacks offers language learning games that are both entertaining and educational. The app includes interactive lessons with vocabulary, grammar, and cultural insights. It features colorful visuals, engaging activities, and quizzes to keep kids motivated and immersed in the language learning process.

These language learning apps provide an interactive and engaging way for school-age kids to develop language skills. Whether it's through gamified lessons, interactive exercises, or mnemonic techniques, these apps offer a fun and effective approach to language acquisition. Encourage your children to explore different languages, embrace cultural diversity, and embark on a linguistic adventure right from their fingertips.

Math and science games: Foster your child's love for numbers and scientific concepts with math and science games. These apps offer interactive challenges, puzzles, and quizzes that make learning math and science entertaining and rewarding. Encourage your kids to solve problems, experiment, and explore the wonders of the world around them.

Here are a few STEM related apps that I always recommend:

1. Khan Academy Kids
   Description: Khan Academy Kids offers a wide range of educational content, including math and science lessons, for children aged 2 to 7. The app provides interactive exercises, games, and videos that cover foundational concepts in an engaging and age-appropriate manner.

2. Prodigy Math Game
   Description: Prodigy Math Game combines math learning with an immersive role-playing game experience. Kids can explore a virtual world, engage in battles, and solve math problems to progress. The app adapts to the child's skill level, providing personalized challenges and tracking their progress.

3. NASA Kids Club
   Description: NASA Kids Club introduces children to the wonders of space and science through interactive games, videos, and activities. Kids can explore the solar system, learn about astronauts, and engage in hands-on experiments while gaining a deeper understanding of STEM concepts.

4. DragonBox Series (DragonBox Numbers, DragonBox Algebra, etc.)
Description: DragonBox offers a series of math apps that make learning algebra, geometry, and numbers intuitive and enjoyable. Through the use of puzzles and visual representations, these apps help kids develop problem-solving skills and build a strong foundation in math.

5. Tynker
Description: Tynker is an app that teaches kids coding and computational thinking skills through game-based activities. Alongside programming concepts, Tynker includes math and science challenges that encourage logical reasoning, problem-solving, and creativity.

These math and science learning apps provide interactive and engaging platforms for school-age kids to develop their STEM skills. From foundational concepts to more advanced topics, these apps combine education with entertainment, making learning an enjoyable and rewarding experience. Encourage your children to explore the wonders of math and science through these interactive tools and watch their knowledge and curiosity thrive.

Geography and history apps: Transform your kids into globe-trotting adventurers with geography and history apps. These apps provide interactive maps, historical timelines, and trivia challenges that help children expand their knowledge of different countries, cultures, and historical events. It's a colorful way to spark curiosity and broaden their understanding of the world.

Bring Geography and History on the road in a super fun way with these captivating apps:

1. National Geographic Kids World Atlas
Description: National Geographic Kids World Atlas app brings geography to life with interactive maps, stunning images, and

fascinating facts about countries, continents, and landmarks. Kids can explore the world's wonders, learn about cultures, and test their knowledge with quizzes and games.

2. Stack the Countries
Description: Stack the Countries is a fun and educational geography app that challenges kids to stack colorful blocks representing different countries. As they answer geography questions correctly, they can unlock new countries and learn interesting facts about each one. The game promotes map recognition, country identification, and geographical knowledge.

3. History Heroes
Description: History Heroes is a captivating app that introduces kids to historical figures and events through interactive card games. Each card features a historical character or event, along with key facts and a trivia game. It's a fun way to learn about important people and moments in history.

4. GeoBee Challenge
Description: GeoBee Challenge is an app based on the National Geographic GeoBee competition. It tests kids' geography knowledge with challenging questions about countries, cities, flags, and more. The app includes multiple-choice quizzes and a world map game to help kids expand their geographic knowledge.

5. Oregon Trail
Description: The Oregon Trail app offers an immersive historical simulation game that teaches kids about the challenges faced by pioneers during the 19th century. Players make decisions, manage resources, and learn about American history as they navigate the trail to the West.

These geography and history apps provide a mix of educational content and interactive gameplay to engage school-age kids in the exploration of our world's past and present. From discovering new countries to uncovering historical events, these apps make learning about geography and history an exciting and immersive experience. Encourage your children to embark on these digital adventures and expand their knowledge of our global and historical heritage.

Kid-friendly movies and TV shows

1. Portable DVD players and tablets: Bring along a portable DVD player or tablet loaded with your kids' favorite movies and TV shows. These devices are perfect for long journeys, providing hours of entertainment. Ensure you have a variety of options to cater to different tastes and ages, allowing your children to indulge in their preferred on-screen adventures.

2. Online streaming services: Access family-friendly movies and TV shows on popular streaming services. Many platforms offer a dedicated section for children's content, featuring a wide range of age-appropriate options. Take advantage of offline viewing features to download shows in advance, ensuring uninterrupted entertainment during areas with limited internet access.

3. Family-friendly movie recommendations: Prepare a list of recommended movies that the whole family can enjoy together. Look for films that offer wholesome entertainment, inspiring themes, and positive messages.

Here are a few of my favorite movies with a theme of adventure to show school age kids along the journey:

1. "Up" (2009)

Description: Follow the heartwarming journey of an elderly widower, Carl Fredricksen, as he embarks on a grand adventure by attaching thousands of balloons to his house. With a young stowaway named Russell, they discover breathtaking landscapes and encounter extraordinary characters, teaching them the true meaning of adventure and friendship.

2. "Moana" (2016)
Description: Join Moana, a spirited young girl, as she sets sail on a daring mission to save her island and discover her own identity. This vibrant and musical Disney film takes viewers on an unforgettable voyage across the ocean, brimming with catchy songs, stunning animation, and the spirit of exploration.

3. "Finding Nemo" (2003)
Description: Dive into the enchanting underwater world with Marlin, a clownfish, as he embarks on an epic journey to find his son, Nemo. This Pixar classic is filled with humor, heart, and breathtaking marine landscapes, introducing viewers to an array of memorable characters along the way.

4. "The Secret Life of Walter Mitty" (2013)
Description: Follow the adventure of Walter Mitty, an ordinary daydreamer, as he embarks on a real-life journey to track down a missing photograph negative. This visually stunning film takes viewers on a global expedition, inspiring them to embrace life's adventures and pursue their dreams.

5. "Around the World in 80 Days" (2004)
Description: Join Phileas Fogg, a British inventor, and his loyal servant, Passepartout, as they race against time to travel across the globe in 80 days. This adventurous comedy takes viewers on a whirlwind tour of exotic locations and offers a lighthearted take on the spirit of exploration.

6. "Rio" (2011)
Description: Fly to the vibrant city of Rio de Janeiro with Blu, a rare macaw, as he embarks on a thrilling journey to find love and save his species from extinction. This animated film immerses viewers in the dazzling landscapes and energetic culture of Brazil, featuring catchy songs and colorful characters.

7. "The Parent Trap" (1998)
Description: Join two identical twins, separated at birth, as they reunite at a summer camp and scheme to bring their divorced parents back together. This heartwarming and comedic film takes viewers on a journey through summer adventures and captures the importance of family and love.

8. "Cars" (2006)
Description: Rev up your engines and join Lightning McQueen, a race car, as he finds himself in a small town called Radiator Springs. This charming Pixar film takes viewers on a cross-country journey, highlighting the beauty of Route 66 and teaching valuable lessons about friendship, humility, and finding joy in the journey.

9. "The Jungle Book" (2016)
Description: Venture into the lush jungles of India with Mowgli, a young boy raised by wolves, as he embarks on a captivating adventure filled with talking animals and magical encounters. This visually stunning live-action adaptation of the classic tale immerses viewers in a world of wonder and self-discovery.

10. "The Princess Diaries" (2001)
Description: Follow the transformation of Mia Thermopolis, an ordinary teenager, as she discovers she is the heir to the throne of a small European kingdom. This charming film takes viewers on a

whimsical journey through royal traditions and self-acceptance, combining comedy, romance, and fairy tale elements.

These movies and TV shows transport school-age kids to captivating worlds, igniting their imagination and sparking their sense of adventure. Whether it's exploring new landscapes, discovering diverse cultures, or embarking on personal journeys, these stories inspire and entertain, leaving lasting impressions and cherished memories. Grab some popcorn, gather the family, and embark on a cinematic journey together!

Virtual reality (VR) experiences

1. VR headsets for kids: Delve into the world of virtual reality with kid-friendly VR headsets. These devices allow children to explore virtual environments and embark on interactive adventures from the comfort of their seats. Look for age-appropriate content and ensure proper fit and usage guidelines for a safe and immersive VR experience.

2. Virtual museum tours and interactive experiences: Transport your family to renowned museums and cultural landmarks with virtual museum tours. Many museums offer online platforms where visitors can explore exhibits, view artwork, and learn about history and culture. Additionally, interactive VR experiences allow children to engage with virtual objects, fostering curiosity and a deeper understanding of the subject matter.

3. Safety considerations for VR usage: While VR can be an incredible tool for entertainment and education, it's essential to prioritize safety. Ensure that children take breaks to rest their eyes and avoid extended periods of VR usage. Set usage guidelines and supervise younger children to ensure they navigate virtual environments responsibly.

With these colorful and engaging technology-based entertainment options, you can enhance your family's travel experience and provide your kids with a world of captivating and educational content. Embrace the wonders of technology, and let your children's imaginations soar as they embark on digital adventures that entertain, educate, and inspire.

Tips for Smooth Traveling: Entertaining Kids During Travel

Traveling with school-age kids can be an exciting and memorable experience, but it's important to be prepared and proactive when it comes to keeping them entertained during the journey. Here are some colorful and engaging tips to ensure a smooth and enjoyable travel experience for the whole family.

Setting realistic expectations

When it comes to entertaining kids during travel, it's essential to set realistic expectations. Understand that there may be moments of restlessness or boredom, especially during long journeys. Instead of aiming for constant entertainment, embrace the opportunity for relaxation and quiet time. Encourage kids to bring along their favorite books, puzzles, or coloring activities to enjoy during these moments. Setting realistic expectations helps create a stress-free environment where everyone can find their own sources of entertainment.

Planning for breaks and downtime

Long journeys can be tiring for kids, so it's important to plan for breaks and downtime. Take advantage of rest areas, airport lounges, or train station waiting areas to stretch, move around, and burn off some energy. Pack a small bag with snacks, water, and a few toys or games to enjoy during these breaks. Providing opportunities for physical activity and refreshment helps kids stay engaged and prevents restlessness.

Involving children in the decision-making process

Empower your kids by involving them in the decision-making process for travel entertainment. Let them choose a selection of books, movies, or games to bring along. Consider creating a travel playlist together with their favorite songs or audiobooks. Engage them in researching fun facts or trivia about the destination, which can spark their curiosity and make the journey more educational and engaging. By involving them, you not only keep them entertained but also foster a sense of ownership and excitement about the trip.

Communicating travel rules and safety guidelines

Before embarking on your journey, it's important to communicate travel rules and safety guidelines to your children. Explain the importance of staying together, following instructions from travel personnel, and respecting the rules of the transportation mode you're using. Ensure they understand the importance of seatbelts, safety in crowded places, and being aware of their belongings. By setting clear guidelines, you create a safe and secure environment for your kids to enjoy their travel experience.

By setting realistic expectations, planning for breaks and downtime, involving children in decision-making, and communicating travel rules and safety guidelines, you can ensure a smooth and enjoyable travel experience for the whole family. Embrace the journey as an opportunity for bonding, exploration, and creating lasting memories. With these colorful tips, you'll be well-prepared to keep your kids entertained and engaged, making the travel experience an adventure to remember.

Chapter 10

Culinary Exploration - Savoring the Flavors of the World

The McDeer family, a group of passionate culinary enthusiasts, embarked on a flavorful adventure to the gastronomic capital of the world—Paris, France. With their taste buds primed and their appetites in full swing, they were ready to indulge in a mouthwatering journey through the city's renowned cuisine.

Their first stop was a charming bakery that boasted an array of delectable pastries. As they entered, the sweet aroma of freshly baked croissants enveloped them, igniting their anticipation. The kids—Julia, Oliver, and Violet—immediately eyed a towering display of colorful macarons, their eyes practically shining with excitement.

Unable to resist the temptation, Mr. McDeer suggested they each choose one macaron to savor. The kids carefully made their selections, deliberating over the vibrant flavors like a panel of judges at a culinary competition.

However, just as they were about to take their first bites, a mischievous gust of wind blew through the bakery, causing Mr. McDeer's map of Paris to flutter from his hands. Chaos ensued as the map flew into the air and gracefully landed on the macarons, effectively sticking to the delicate treats like edible post-it notes.

The McDeer family stared in disbelief at the comical scene before them—a macaron mosaic of sticky paper and vibrant colors. The bakery patrons erupted into laughter, and even the baker couldn't help but chuckle at the whimsical art installation that had unwittingly unfolded.

The McDeer kids, not ones to let an opportunity for creativity pass them by, took it upon themselves to name each macaron according to the areas of Paris indicated on the map. "I'll have the Montmartre macaron," declared Julia, pointing to a bright red one with a tiny piece of the map sticking out.

Amidst laughter and sticky fingers, the McDeer family savored their unique and unintentional fusion of art and cuisine. They snapped photos of their "map-arons" and shared them with friends back home, transforming an unexpected mishap into a whimsical souvenir of their Parisian culinary escapades.

Throughout the rest of their adventure in Paris, the McDeer family continued to encounter amusing and delicious moments. From playfully attempting French pronunciations to indulging in decadent cheese platters, their love for food and laughter intertwined, creating an unforgettable tapestry of flavors and memories.

As they bid adieu to the City of Lights, the McDeer family carried with them not only memories of Paris' gastronomic wonders but also a story of their map-arons—a reminder of the joy that comes from embracing unexpected moments and finding humor in culinary adventures gone slightly awry.

In this chapter, we invite you to embark on a gastronomic adventure as we explore the joys of introducing your children to diverse cuisines. From local street food to fine dining experiences, we will show you how to expand their palates and create a lifelong appreciation for culinary delights.

Importance of introducing children to diverse cuisines:

As parents, we play a crucial role in shaping our children's perspectives and exposing them to new experiences. Introducing them to diverse cuisines is an essential part of this journey. Food is not merely sustenance; it is a gateway to understanding different cultures, traditions, and ways of life. By encouraging our children to explore culinary delights from around the world, we give them the opportunity to develop a broader worldview and a deeper appreciation for diversity.

Benefits of expanding their palates:

Expanding your child's palate goes beyond simply encouraging them to try new foods. It opens up a world of flavors, textures, and aromas that stimulate their senses and enhance their dining experiences. By exposing them to a wide variety of cuisines, you can help them develop a more adventurous and flexible approach to food, making them less picky eaters and more willing to embrace new culinary experiences.

Creating a lifelong appreciation for culinary delights:

By fostering a love for diverse cuisines in your children, you are nurturing a lifelong appreciation for culinary delights. This appreciation extends beyond the mere act of eating; it encompasses an understanding of the cultural significance, history, and artistry that goes into creating each dish. It empowers your children to seek out new flavors, explore different culinary traditions, and engage in meaningful conversations about food. This appreciation for culinary delights will stay with them throughout their lives, enhancing their travel experiences and broadening their horizons.

In the following chapters, we will guide you through various aspects of culinary exploration with your children. From discovering local street food to participating in cooking classes, we will provide practical tips, recommendations, and insights to help you make the most of your culinary adventures. So, fasten your seatbelts and get ready to savor the flavors of the world together with your children!

Preparing for the Culinary Adventure

Get ready to dive into a world of delicious flavors and mouthwatering delights! Before you embark on your culinary adventure with your school-age children, it's important to make some preparations to ensure a smooth and enjoyable experience. Let's explore how you can get ready to savor the flavors of the world together:

Researching Local Cuisines:

The first step in preparing for your culinary adventure is to research the local cuisines of your destination. What are the signature dishes and culinary traditions that make the region unique? Take the time to familiarize yourself with the flavors, ingredients, and cooking techniques that you and your children will encounter. This will not only enhance your appreciation for the food but also allow you to have informed discussions with your little food enthusiasts.

Identifying Child-Friendly Restaurants and Eateries:

Traveling with children means finding restaurants and eateries that cater to their needs. Look for child-friendly establishments that provide a welcoming atmosphere and menus with options suitable for young taste buds. Seek out places that offer kid-sized portions, colorful presentations, or interactive dining experiences. Reading reviews and recommendations from fellow travelers can be a great way to discover the best dining spots that will delight both you and your little ones.

Understanding Dietary Restrictions and Allergies:

When traveling with school-age children, it's important to be mindful of any dietary restrictions or allergies they may have. Take the time to understand their specific needs and seek out restaurants that can accommodate those requirements. Be prepared to communicate any dietary restrictions to restaurant staff and ask for recommendations or modifications if necessary. Remember, the safety and well-being of your children come first, so it's essential to plan ahead and ensure their dietary needs are met.

Planning Meals and Snacks Accordingly:

To keep your energy levels up during your culinary adventure, it's important to plan meals and snacks accordingly. Consider the timing of your activities and plan for regular breaks to enjoy delicious meals together. Research restaurants or food stalls that align with your itinerary, allowing you to conveniently satisfy your cravings. Additionally, packing some nutritious and easily portable snacks can come in handy during long days of exploration. Having a variety of options on hand will help keep hunger at bay and ensure everyone stays happy and satisfied.

By taking the time to research local cuisines, identify child-friendly establishments, understand dietary restrictions, and plan meals and snacks accordingly, you'll set the stage for a fantastic culinary adventure with your school-age children. So, get ready to embark on a flavorful journey and create lasting memories as you savor the diverse culinary delights awaiting you at your destination!

Exploring Local Street Food

Get ready to tantalize your taste buds and dive into the vibrant world of local street food! When traveling with school-age children, exploring the exciting realm of street food can be an unforgettable experience. Let's hit the streets and embark on a culinary adventure together:

Introduction to the Concept of Street Food:
Street food is like a portal to the heart and soul of a city. It's the perfect fusion of flavors, aromas, and culinary traditions that come together to

create unique and delicious dishes. Explaining the concept of street food to your children is like opening a treasure chest of culinary wonders. Street food vendors set up shop on the sidewalks, bustling markets, or vibrant food stalls, offering quick and delectable bites that showcase the local food culture. From mouthwatering tacos to savory dumplings, the world of street food is a feast for the senses.

Sampling Popular Street Food Dishes in Different Regions:

As you venture into the world of street food, encourage your children to embrace the spirit of adventure and try new flavors. Each region boasts its own signature street food dishes, so make it a point to sample the local specialties wherever you go. In Southeast Asia, you can savor the aromatic delights of Pad Thai in Thailand, flavorful satay skewers in Malaysia, or steaming bowls of pho in Vietnam. In Mexico, indulge in the spicy goodness of tacos al pastor or treat your taste buds to the zesty flavors of ceviche in Peru. By exploring different regions and sampling their street food, you and your children will embark on a culinary journey that spans the globe.

Ensuring Food Safety and Hygiene While Enjoying Street Food:

While immersing yourself in the street food scene, it's crucial to prioritize food safety and hygiene. Look for vendors who follow good food handling practices, such as using gloves, maintaining clean cooking surfaces, and handling food with care. Opt for stalls or carts where you can see the food being freshly prepared. It's also important to ensure that the ingredients are fresh and cooked thoroughly. By being mindful of food safety, you can fully enjoy the delectable street food while keeping any worries at bay.

Teaching Children about Cultural Significance and Traditions Related to Street Food:

Street food is not just about satisfying hunger; it's deeply rooted in cultural significance and traditions. Use this opportunity to teach your children about the history and customs surrounding street food in each destination. Share stories about the origins of specific dishes, the role they play in local celebrations or festivals, and the cultural significance attached to them. For example, in Japan, they have the lively tradition of yatai stalls at festivals, where children can sample delicious takoyaki or yakisoba while soaking in the festive atmosphere. By understanding the cultural context, your children will develop a deeper appreciation for the culinary heritage of the places they visit.

When it comes to street food, some cities around the world are renowned for their culinary delights. Here are ten cities that are celebrated for offering some of the best street food experiences:

1. Bangkok, Thailand: Known for its bustling street markets and vibrant food stalls, Bangkok is a haven for street food enthusiasts. Indulge in flavorsome Pad Thai, spicy Tom Yum soup, savory satay skewers, and an array of delicious Thai snacks.

2. Istanbul, Turkey: Istanbul's streets are filled with the enticing aromas of Turkish street food. Savor mouthwatering kebabs, fragrant Turkish tea, fresh seafood sandwiches, and delectable pastries like baklava and simit.

3. Mexico City, Mexico: Mexican street food is famous worldwide, and Mexico City takes it to a whole new level. Dive into flavorful tacos, quesadillas, tamales, and churros. Don't forget to try the tantalizing street corn topped with cheese, lime, and spices.

4. Marrakech, Morocco: The bustling souks of Marrakech are a street food paradise. Savor the aromatic tagines, indulge in tender lamb skewers, sample savory Moroccan pastries like pastilla, and sip on refreshing mint tea.

5. Hanoi, Vietnam: Hanoi's vibrant street food scene is a treat for the taste buds. Try the iconic pho noodle soup, crispy Banh Mi sandwiches, delectable Vietnamese spring rolls, and rich egg coffee.

6. Penang, Malaysia: Penang is a food lover's dream, blending Malay, Chinese, and Indian culinary influences. Explore the bustling hawker centers and savor dishes like Char Kway Teow (stir-fried noodles), Nasi Lemak (coconut rice), and Assam Laksa (spicy noodle soup).

7. Mumbai, India: Mumbai is famous for its street food culture, known locally as "chaat." Treat yourself to mouthwatering vada pav (spicy potato fritters), pani puri (crispy hollow shells filled with tangy water), and buttery pav bhaji (mixed vegetable curry served with bread).

8. Seoul, South Korea: Seoul's street food scene is a delightful fusion of flavors. Try the popular Korean street food snacks such as tteokbokki (spicy rice cakes), Korean-style fried chicken, savory gimbap (rice rolls), and hotteok (sweet pancakes).

9. New York City, USA: The Big Apple offers a diverse array of street food from around the world. From iconic hot dogs and pretzels to halal carts serving mouthwatering kebabs, falafel, and flavorful tacos, NYC is a street food paradise.

10. Singapore: Singapore's hawker centers are legendary, showcasing an incredible variety of street food. Savor the aromatic Hainanese chicken rice, flavorful laksa, succulent chili crab, and delectable roti prata.

These cities are just a taste of the street food wonders awaiting you around the world. Each offers its own unique flavors, culinary traditions, and vibrant street food culture that will leave you and your children with unforgettable culinary memories.

So, get ready to roam the bustling streets and let the enticing aromas guide you to mouthwatering delights. Exploring local street food is not just about the food itself; it's about immersing yourselves in the rich tapestry of flavors, cultures, and traditions that make each destination unique. Open up your senses, embrace the adventure, and create lasting memories as you indulge in the tantalizing world of street food with your school-age children. Bon appétit!

Visiting Local Markets and Food Halls

Welcome to a bustling world of sights, sounds, and flavors! As you travel with your school-age children, one experience you simply can't miss is visiting the vibrant local markets and food halls. These lively hubs are a treasure trove of culinary wonders, offering a sensory feast that will delight both young and old. Let's dive into this colorful adventure together:

Exploring Vibrant Local Markets:

Step into a world where colors come alive, where the aroma of spices fills the air, and where the energy of the locals is contagious. Local markets are vibrant hubs of activity, where vendors proudly display their bountiful produce, fragrant spices, and enticing street food. Encourage your children to explore these markets, meandering through rows of stalls, taking in the vibrant atmosphere, and immersing themselves in the local culture. From sprawling outdoor markets to covered food halls, each destination holds its own unique charm waiting to be discovered.

Encouraging Children to Interact with Local Vendors:
Engaging with the local vendors is an excellent opportunity for your children to learn about the food and culture directly from the source. Encourage them to strike up conversations with the vendors, asking about the ingredients, the cooking methods, and even the stories behind

their recipes. Many vendors take pride in their culinary heritage and will happily share their knowledge and passion. Through these interactions, your children will develop a deeper appreciation for the food and the people who bring it to life.

Explaining the Importance of Fresh and Seasonal Ingredients:

One of the most valuable lessons your children can learn at local markets is the importance of fresh and seasonal ingredients. As you browse through the stalls, point out the vibrant fruits, crisp vegetables, and fragrant herbs that are in season. Explain how using locally sourced and fresh ingredients enhances the flavors of the dishes. Teach them to appreciate the difference that quality ingredients can make, fostering a love for fresh, wholesome food that will stay with them for years to come.

Sampling Local Produce and Specialty Items:

Local markets offer an array of tantalizing produce and specialty items that are unique to the region. Encourage your children to try a variety of fruits, perhaps introducing them to exotic flavors they've never experienced before. Let them sample regional specialties such as cheeses, cured meats, spices, or baked goods. By encouraging them to be adventurous with their taste buds, you'll open up a world of flavors and textures that will create lasting memories.

Discovering Unique Flavors and Ingredients:

Local markets are treasure troves of unique flavors and ingredients waiting to be discovered. Encourage your children to keep an eye out for unusual spices, herbs, or condiments that they can bring back home as culinary souvenirs. Let them explore the diverse array of ingredients and challenge them to find something they've never seen before. This way, you'll not only introduce them to new flavors but also inspire their creativity in the kitchen.

There are so many incredible cities around the world, typically abroad, that offer market culture at its finest. Here are a few of my favorites:

1. Marrakech, Morocco: Marrakech's vibrant medinas and bustling souks offer a sensory overload of colors, scents, and flavors. Explore the lively marketplaces, such as Jemaa el-Fnaa, and immerse yourself in Moroccan culture through a variety of spices, textiles, ceramics, and traditional crafts.

2. Istanbul, Turkey: Istanbul's bazaars, like the Grand Bazaar and Spice Bazaar, are legendary. Lose yourself in a labyrinth of stalls selling everything from colorful spices and Turkish tea sets to exquisite rugs and ceramics. Don't forget to haggle and sip on traditional Turkish tea as you navigate these bustling marketplaces.

3. Chiang Mai, Thailand: Chiang Mai's famous Night Bazaar is a paradise for shoppers and food lovers alike. Sample delicious Thai street food, browse through stalls offering handcrafted items, and soak up the vibrant atmosphere of this bustling outdoor market.

4. Jaipur, India: Known as the Pink City, Jaipur is home to vibrant bazaars filled with textiles, jewelry, and handicrafts. The bustling markets of Johari Bazaar and Bapu Bazaar are perfect for shopping for intricately designed fabrics, colorful turbans, and precious gemstones.

5. Fez, Morocco: The medieval city of Fez is renowned for its ancient medina, which hosts one of the world's largest pedestrian-only urban areas. Explore the maze-like streets, marvel at the skilled artisans crafting leather goods and intricate ceramics, and immerse yourself in the vibrant market atmosphere.

6. Hoi An, Vietnam: Hoi An's UNESCO-listed Ancient Town is a treasure trove of market stalls and traditional shops. Discover local handicrafts, tailor-made clothing, and sample mouthwatering Vietnamese street food in this charming and well-preserved city.

7. Oaxaca City, Mexico: Oaxaca's markets are a celebration of Mexican culture and cuisine. Visit the bustling Mercado Benito Juarez to find an array of fresh produce, local spices, traditional textiles, and handmade crafts. Don't miss out on trying regional specialties like mole and mezcal.

8. Cusco, Peru: Cusco's San Pedro Market is a vibrant and bustling place to explore. Sample exotic fruits, try traditional Peruvian snacks, and browse through the market's stalls offering textiles, handicrafts, and local produce. It's also a great spot to shop for unique souvenirs.

9. Ubud, Bali, Indonesia: Ubud's art markets offer a glimpse into Balinese culture and craftsmanship. Stroll through the market stalls, filled with intricate wood carvings, traditional paintings, handmade jewelry, and vibrant textiles. It's the perfect place to find unique treasures and support local artisans.

These cities showcase the incredible outdoor market cultures found around the world. Each offers a distinct blend of sights, sounds, and products, providing a rich cultural experience and an opportunity to immerse yourself in the local way of life.

So, get ready to immerse yourselves in the vibrant tapestry of local markets and food halls. Let the colors, aromas, and flavors guide you on a captivating journey. Encourage your school-age children to interact with local vendors, explore the importance of fresh ingredients, and indulge in unique flavors and produce. By experiencing the magic of local markets together, you'll create unforgettable memories and instill in your children a love for culinary exploration that will last a lifetime. Happy market-hopping!

Hands-On Experiences: Cooking Classes and Food Tours

Get ready to put on your aprons and embark on a flavorful journey through cooking classes and food tours! These hands-on experiences offer an exciting way for parents and their school-age children to immerse themselves in the world of culinary delights. Let's explore the joys of cooking and the exploration of culinary heritage together:

Participating in Family-Friendly Cooking Classes:
Cooking classes provide a fantastic opportunity for families to bond, learn, and create delicious memories together. Seek out family-friendly cooking classes in your destination, where experienced chefs will guide you through the preparation of traditional dishes. From rolling sushi in Japan to making fresh pasta in Italy, these classes allow your children to develop new culinary skills while gaining a deeper understanding of the local cuisine.

Learning to Prepare Traditional Dishes from Different Cultures:

One of the greatest joys of cooking classes is the chance to learn and prepare traditional dishes from different cultures. Expand your family's culinary horizons as you discover the secrets of creating authentic flavors. From mastering the art of making Indian curries to learning the technique behind French pastries, these classes allow you to bring the world's cuisines into your own kitchen.

Engaging Children in the Cooking Process:

Cooking is not just about the end result; it's about the journey. Encourage your children to actively participate in the cooking process. Let them chop, mix, and stir, allowing them to feel a sense of ownership over the meal. By involving them in the preparation, you empower them to develop a love for cooking and a sense of accomplishment as they contribute to the family feast.

Taking Food Tours to Explore Culinary Heritage and Traditions:

Food tours are a delicious adventure for the entire family. Join a guided tour that takes you through local markets, street food stalls, and hidden gems, allowing you to discover the culinary heritage and traditions of your destination. Taste regional specialties, learn about the history of the dishes, and engage with local vendors and artisans who are passionate about their craft.

Encouraging Children to Ask Questions and Learn about the History of the Dishes:

Food is not just about flavors and ingredients; it is a reflection of history, culture, and traditions. Encourage your children to ask questions during cooking classes and food tours. Engage in conversations with chefs, vendors, and tour guides to learn about the origins and stories behind the dishes you're preparing or sampling. This will not only deepen their appreciation for the food but also foster their curiosity about different cultures and culinary customs.

So, tie on your aprons, embark on cooking adventures, and let your taste buds guide you on food tours. Embrace the opportunity to learn, create, and explore the culinary heritage of the places you visit. Through cooking classes and food tours, you'll not only create delectable dishes but also cultivate a lifelong passion for food, culture, and the stories that bring them together.

Fine Dining with a Twist

Get ready to embark on a culinary adventure that combines elegance with a touch of whimsy as we explore fine dining with a twist. Contrary to popular belief, fine dining experiences can be just as enjoyable for parents traveling with school-age children. Let's discover how you can introduce your little ones to the world of refined gastronomy while keeping the experience fun and engaging:

Introducing Children to Fine Dining Experiences:
Fine dining is not just reserved for adults; it can be a wonderful opportunity to expose children to new flavors, culinary techniques, and dining experiences. By introducing your children to fine dining, you expand their palates, stimulate their senses, and teach them to appreciate the artistry and attention to detail that goes into creating exceptional dishes.

Exploring Child-Friendly Fine Dining Options:

When seeking fine dining experiences with children, it's essential to find child-friendly establishments that cater to their needs. Look for restaurants that offer a welcoming atmosphere, attentive staff, and menus designed with younger taste buds in mind. Some establishments even offer special kids' menus or creative presentations that add an element of fun to the dining experience. Research and read reviews to discover the best child-friendly fine dining options at your destination.

Teaching Dining Etiquette and Table Manners:

Fine dining experiences provide an excellent opportunity to teach your children proper dining etiquette and table manners. Before you go, have a conversation about the importance of being respectful and polite in a fine dining setting. Guide them on the basics, such as using utensils properly, sitting up straight, and engaging in conversation with those at the table. Encourage them to observe and learn from the behavior of fellow diners, and reinforce positive dining habits throughout the meal.

Encouraging Children to Try New Flavors and Dishes:

Fine dining experiences often present an array of unique flavors and dishes. Encourage your children to embrace the adventure by trying new flavors and expanding their culinary horizons. Encourage them to be open-minded and explore the full range of flavors and textures presented on their plates. Support their curiosity and help them identify and describe the different tastes and ingredients they encounter. By doing so, you empower them to develop a sense of culinary exploration and broaden their culinary repertoire.

So, get ready to elevate your dining experiences and venture into the world of fine dining with your school-age children. From elegantly presented dishes to the delight of trying new flavors, fine dining with a twist promises a culinary journey like no other. By introducing your children to refined dining experiences and encouraging them to embrace new flavors and dishes, you open the door to a lifetime of culinary appreciation and a world of gastronomic possibilities.

Catering to Dietary Restrictions and Allergies

When traveling with school-age children, it's important to ensure that their dietary restrictions and allergies are well-catered to. Fortunately, with a little preparation and research, you can navigate the culinary landscape with ease. Let's dive into how you can accommodate your children's dietary needs while still savoring the flavors of your destination:

Understanding Common Dietary Restrictions and Allergies:
First and foremost, familiarize yourself with common dietary restrictions and allergies that your children may have. Whether it's gluten-free, lactose intolerance, nut allergies, or any other dietary restriction, having a clear understanding of their needs will guide you in making appropriate food choices. This knowledge will help you identify potential challenges and seek suitable alternatives while exploring local cuisine.

Researching Child-Friendly Restaurants with Accommodating Menus:

Before you embark on your journey, conduct thorough research to identify child-friendly restaurants that offer accommodating menus. Many establishments nowadays provide options for different dietary needs, making it easier to find meals that align with your children's restrictions. Look for restaurants with clearly marked allergen information or menus that specify gluten-free, vegetarian, or other dietary options. Reading reviews and recommendations from other travelers can also provide insights into suitable dining venues.

Communicating Dietary Needs to Restaurant Staff:

Once you've chosen a restaurant, it's important to communicate your children's dietary needs to the restaurant staff. Whether it's informing them about allergies, restrictions, or specific ingredients to avoid, clear and open communication is key. Don't hesitate to ask questions about the preparation methods, cross-contamination risks, or ingredient substitutions. By proactively discussing your children's needs with the staff, you can ensure that their meals are prepared safely and in accordance with their dietary requirements.

Seeking Local Advice for Suitable Dining Options:

While researching and planning your trip, reach out to locals or seek advice from reliable sources about suitable dining options for your children's dietary needs. Locals can provide valuable insights into hidden gems or specialty restaurants that are known for catering to specific dietary restrictions. Additionally, they may be able to recommend local dishes or ingredients that are naturally free from allergens or suitable for certain dietary preferences.

Remember, catering to your children's dietary restrictions and allergies doesn't mean missing out on the culinary delights of your destination. With careful planning, effective communication, and local advice, you can find suitable dining options that accommodate their needs without compromising on taste and experience. By ensuring their dietary requirements are met, you can enjoy your travel adventures with peace of mind and create a memorable culinary journey for the whole family.

Safety Tips for Culinary Exploration

Culinary exploration is a thrilling adventure, but it's essential to prioritize safety and well-being while indulging in the flavors of the world. As you travel with your school-age children, here are some colorful and engaging tips to ensure a safe and enjoyable culinary experience:

Teaching Children about Food Safety and Hygiene:
Before embarking on your culinary journey, make sure to teach your children about food safety and hygiene. Show them the importance of washing hands thoroughly before meals and after handling raw foods. Explain the significance of clean utensils and surfaces in preventing foodborne illnesses. By instilling these habits, you empower your children to make informed choices and enjoy their culinary adventures while staying safe and healthy.

Choosing Reputable Restaurants and Eateries:
When dining out, it's crucial to choose reputable restaurants and eateries that prioritize food safety and quality. Look for establishments with excellent hygiene standards, visible cleanliness, and positive reviews from trusted sources. Consider seeking recommendations from locals or fellow travelers who have had positive experiences. By selecting reliable establishments, you can relax and enjoy your meals, knowing that the food is prepared and served with utmost care.

Being Cautious about Street Food Vendors and Food Stalls:

Street food is a fantastic way to experience the local flavors and culture, but it's important to exercise caution. Before indulging in street food, look for vendors and stalls that practice good food handling and hygiene. Opt for stalls where food is cooked fresh and served hot. Pay attention to cleanliness, such as the vendor's personal hygiene and the overall cleanliness of the stall. Trust your instincts, and if something doesn't seem right, it's best to err on the side of caution. By being vigilant and selective, you can savor the delicious street food while minimizing any potential risks.

Managing Portion Sizes and Maintaining a Balanced Diet:

Culinary exploration often involves indulging in a variety of delectable dishes, but it's important to manage portion sizes and maintain a balanced diet. Encourage your children to appreciate the flavors while being mindful of their hunger cues. Share dishes as a family, allowing everyone to sample a variety of flavors without overindulging. Additionally, balance out rich or heavy meals with lighter options and incorporate fresh fruits and vegetables into your diet. By promoting moderation and balance, you ensure that your culinary adventures contribute to a healthy lifestyle.

Remember, safety is paramount during your culinary exploration. By teaching your children about food safety and hygiene, choosing reputable establishments, being cautious with street food, and managing portion sizes, you can create a safe and enjoyable experience for the whole family. Embrace the diverse flavors of the world while prioritizing well-being, and embark on a culinary journey that will be both scrumptious and memorable. Bon appétit and happy and safe travels!

Chapter 11

Safety and Health - Ensuring a Secure Journey

The Hayes family, including their mischievous twin girls, Charlotte and Blaine, embarked on a magical journey to the enchanting realm of Disney World in Orlando, Florida. With their Mickey Mouse ears donned and excitement in their eyes, they were ready for an adventure of a lifetime.

Their first stop was the iconic Cinderella Castle at the heart of the Magic Kingdom. As they stood in awe of the majestic structure, little Charlotte couldn't contain her enthusiasm and decided to give the castle a big, affectionate hug.

To her surprise—and the amusement of her family—a cast member dressed as Cinderella's Fairy Godmother witnessed the adorable gesture. In the blink of an eye, she appeared before Charlotte, waved her wand, and exclaimed, "Oh, my dear, you have brought the castle to life with your magical hug!"

The Johnson family watched in disbelief as the castle began to emit a vibrant glow, transforming into a spectacle of twinkling lights. The crowd gathered around, their cameras clicking away, capturing the extraordinary moment.

Blaine, not one to be outdone by her sister, turned to a nearby lamppost and shouted, "You're next, Mr. Lamppost!" much to the amusement of the surrounding visitors. They chuckled and cheered Blaine on, half-expecting the lamppost to come alive with magic.

As the Hayes family continued their adventure through Disney World, their mischievous antics and contagious laughter filled the air. Charlotte and Blaine insisted on "testing" the rides by giggling loudly and declaring them "kid-approved" after each exhilarating experience.

During the Pirates of the Caribbean ride, the mischievous twins even tried to recruit the animatronic pirates into their imaginary crew, waving their plastic swords and offering them "pirate training" tips. Their enthusiasm and imaginative play infected the other riders, turning the boat into a swashbuckling escapade.

As the day wore on, the Johnson family roamed from park to park, embracing every moment of Disney magic. They danced with their favorite characters, sang along with parade performers, and indulged in Mickey-shaped treats that left their faces delightfully smeared with chocolate.

At the end of the day, as the fireworks lit up the sky above Cinderella Castle, the Hayes family huddled together, their hearts brimming with joy. They reveled in the memories they had created, the laughter that had echoed through the parks, and the undeniable magic that had seeped into every moment.

As they bid farewell to Disney World, Charlotte and Blaine couldn't help but whisper to each other, "When can we go on another magical adventure?" And the Hayes parents, sharing a knowing smile, knew that their mischievous twin girls had already begun plotting their next escapade—wherever it may be, laughter and enchantment were sure to follow.

As you embark on unforgettable adventures with your school-age children, their safety and well-being become of utmost priority. In this chapter, we'll dive into the essential topic of Safety and Health, equipping you with expert advice to ensure a secure journey for your entire family.

Picture this: you and your little explorers wandering through vibrant markets in far-flung destinations, immersing yourselves in diverse cultures, and creating treasured memories together. But amidst the exhilaration and wonder, it's crucial to remember that a happy journey is a safe journey.

We've crafted this chapter to be your compass, guiding you through the intricate web of safety considerations, health precautions, and emergency preparedness. From travel vaccinations to health insurance and everything in between, we've got you covered.

So, whether you're planning a trip to a tropical paradise, a historical city, or a breathtaking natural wonder, fasten your seatbelts and get ready to embark on a colorful and informative journey into the realm of ensuring your family's safety and well-being.

Together, we'll unravel the mysteries of travel vaccinations, empowering you to protect your loved ones from potential health risks. We'll navigate the complex world of health insurance, ensuring you have the coverage you need for peace of mind. And we'll dive deep into emergency preparedness, arming you with the knowledge and resources to handle any unforeseen circumstances with confidence.

Throughout this chapter, our goal is to help you create a secure and worry-free environment, where your focus can be on the joy of exploration and the magic of shared experiences. We believe that with the right information and proactive measures, you can ensure that every step of your journey is taken with utmost care.

So, let's embark on this adventure together, where safety and health become our steadfast companions. By the end of this chapter, you'll feel empowered and ready to conquer the world, knowing that you have the tools to safeguard your family's well-being throughout your incredible travels.

Are you ready? Let's dive in and discover the secrets to a secure journey that will make your trip truly unforgettable!

Understanding Travel Vaccinations

Imagine stepping into a world of vibrant cultures, stunning landscapes, and captivating adventures with your school-age children. As you plan your international escapades, one crucial aspect to consider is travel vaccinations – the key to unlocking a worry-free journey. In this section, we'll delve into the importance of travel vaccinations, how to research destination-specific requirements, schedule appointments with healthcare professionals, and manage any potential side effects or reactions.

The Importance of Travel Vaccinations for International Trips

Before your family sets off on a globetrotting expedition, it's vital to understand the significance of travel vaccinations. These little superheroes in vial form shield your loved ones from preventable diseases that may lurk in different corners of the world. They act as a shield, fortifying their immune systems and ensuring a healthy voyage. By staying up-to-date on vaccinations, you not only safeguard your family but also contribute to global health by preventing the spread of contagious diseases.

Researching Destination-Specific Vaccination Requirements and Recommendations

Every destination has its own unique set of health risks and immunization requirements. Just as you plan the exciting activities and sightseeing, dedicate some time to research the specific vaccinations recommended or mandated for your chosen location. Government health websites, travel clinics, and reputable travel guides are excellent resources for up-to-date information. Discover the necessary vaccines to keep your family safe and healthy during your adventures.

Scheduling Appointments with Healthcare Professionals and Understanding the Vaccination Process

Armed with knowledge about destination-specific vaccination requirements, it's time to partner with healthcare professionals. Schedule appointments with your family doctor, travel clinic, or specialized travel health provider well in advance of your trip. These experts will guide you through the vaccination process, ensuring you receive the necessary immunizations for your destination and travel itinerary.

During the appointment, share your travel plans and itinerary, including any specific activities or regions you'll be exploring. Your healthcare provider will tailor their advice to your family's needs, considering factors such as your children's ages, current immunization status, and individual health considerations. They'll explain the benefits, potential side effects, and any necessary precautions for each recommended vaccine.

Managing Any Potential Side Effects or Reactions

While travel vaccinations are essential, it's normal to have concerns about potential side effects or reactions. Remember, the majority of side effects are mild and temporary, such as redness or soreness at the injection site, low-grade fever, or mild fatigue. These are signs that the body's immune system is building protection against the targeted diseases.

To ease any worries, ask your healthcare provider about common side effects and how to manage them. They may suggest over-the-counter pain relievers, applying a cold compress, or simply rest and hydration. Being aware of potential reactions and having a plan in place will give you peace of mind and allow you to support your children comfortably throughout the vaccination process.

By understanding the importance of travel vaccinations, researching destination-specific requirements, scheduling appointments with healthcare professionals, and managing potential side effects or reactions, you'll become a confident guardian of your family's health. With each immunization, you unlock new doors to unforgettable experiences, knowing that your loved ones are protected against preventable diseases. So, roll up those sleeves, embrace the power of vaccinations, and embark on a safe and extraordinary journey together!

Securing Health Insurance When Traveling Abroad

Welcome to the section on securing health insurance, where we dive into the world of comprehensive coverage for your international adventures with your school-age children. As you embark on exciting journeys, it's crucial to prioritize the well-being of your family. In this section, we'll explore the importance of adequate health insurance coverage, evaluating existing plans, researching travel insurance options, and understanding the terms and conditions of the chosen insurance plan.

Importance of Adequate Health Insurance Coverage for International Travel

Picture this: your family, wide-eyed with wonder, exploring vibrant markets, ancient ruins, and breathtaking landscapes in a far-off land. While travel promises incredible experiences, it's essential to acknowledge the unexpected. Adequate health insurance coverage becomes your safety net, ensuring that unforeseen medical expenses don't dampen your spirits. From minor mishaps to more serious emergencies, the right insurance plan provides peace of mind, allowing you to focus on the joy of exploration.

Evaluating Existing Health Insurance Plans and Determining if Additional Coverage is Necessary

Before jetting off to distant horizons, take a moment to evaluate your existing health insurance plans. Some policies offer limited or no coverage outside your home country, leaving you vulnerable to exorbitant medical bills. Check with your insurance provider to understand the extent of coverage during international travel.

If your current plan falls short, consider supplementing it with additional coverage. Some insurance companies offer specific travel insurance add-ons or policies tailored for international journeys. By filling the gaps in your existing coverage, you can ensure that your family receives comprehensive protection throughout your travels.

Researching Travel Insurance Options that Provide Comprehensive Health Coverage

To embark on your adventures fully prepared, it's time to explore the world of travel insurance. Research reputable insurance providers who specialize in comprehensive health coverage for travelers. Look for policies that include emergency medical expenses, hospitalization, medical evacuation, and repatriation. These features become invaluable in times of unforeseen medical emergencies, providing a safety net that spans continents.

Consider the specific needs of your family. Are you engaging in any high-risk activities or sports during your trip? Ensure that your insurance policy covers such activities, providing a safety net for any mishaps that might occur.

Understanding the Terms and Conditions of the Chosen Insurance Plan

As you narrow down your choices and select a travel insurance plan, take the time to read and understand the terms and conditions. Pay attention to coverage limits, deductibles, pre-existing conditions, and any exclusions that may apply. Familiarize yourself with the claims process and the necessary documentation you may need in case of an emergency. Understanding the fine print allows you to make informed decisions and prevents surprises should the need for medical assistance arise.

Remember, knowledge is power. By securing adequate health insurance coverage, you become a guardian of your family's well-being during your adventures. Evaluate your existing plans, supplement coverage if needed, research comprehensive travel insurance options, and understand the terms and conditions of your chosen plan. With each step, you build a protective shield around your family, allowing you to embrace the wonders of travel with confidence and peace of mind.

So, take a moment to secure the safety net, ensuring that your family's health remains a top priority throughout your thrilling journeys. With comprehensive health insurance coverage, you're ready to embark on a worry-free expedition, knowing that you have the support you need, no matter where in the world your adventures take you!

Emergency Preparedness - Your Guide to Peace of Mind

Welcome to the section on emergency preparedness, where we equip you with the knowledge and tools to ensure a safe and secure journey for your family as you explore the world with your school-age children. From unforeseen bumps along the road to unexpected twists in your adventures, being prepared is the key to maintaining peace of mind. In this section, we'll cover creating a comprehensive emergency plan, identifying essential contact information, packing a well-stocked first aid kit, and familiarizing yourself with local emergency services and medical facilities.

Creating a Comprehensive Emergency Plan Before Departure

Every journey begins with a plan, and when it comes to emergency preparedness, having a comprehensive plan in place is essential. Gather your family and discuss the necessary steps to take in case of an emergency. Designate meeting points, establish communication protocols, and ensure everyone understands the importance of staying calm and following instructions. By proactively addressing potential emergency scenarios, you empower your family to navigate through challenging situations with confidence and unity.

Identifying Emergency Contact Information for Medical Services and Local Authorities

Before setting foot in a new destination, it's crucial to be armed with the knowledge of who to contact in case of emergencies. Research and note down the emergency contact numbers for local medical services and authorities. These numbers vary from country to country, so make sure to have them readily available in your phone, written down, or stored in a travel app. In times of need, having the right contact information at your fingertips can make all the difference.

Packing a Well-Stocked First Aid Kit and Essential Medications

When it comes to emergency preparedness, a well-stocked first aid kit becomes your family's trusty companion. Pack it with colorful bandages, antiseptic wipes, adhesive tape, tweezers, and other essentials. Don't forget to include any necessary medications your family members may require during the trip. Check expiration dates, refill prescriptions, and ensure you have an adequate supply to last the duration of your journey. With a properly stocked first aid kit and necessary medications, you'll be ready to tackle minor injuries and illnesses that may arise.

Familiarizing Yourself with Local Emergency Services and Medical Facilities at Your Destination

Just as you familiarize yourself with the exciting attractions and activities at your destination, take the time to research and understand the local emergency services and medical facilities. Note the locations of hospitals, clinics, and pharmacies near your accommodation or popular tourist areas. Familiarize yourself with any specific protocols or requirements for accessing medical services in your destination country. By knowing the lay of the land, you can swiftly navigate through any unforeseen medical situations and seek assistance promptly.

Remember, preparation is the key to peace of mind. By creating a comprehensive emergency plan, identifying essential contact information, packing a well-stocked first aid kit, and familiarizing yourself with local emergency services and medical facilities, you become a proactive guardian of your family's well-being. These simple yet crucial steps ensure that you're ready to face any unforeseen challenges and keep your family safe during your travels.

So, embark on your journey with confidence, knowing that you're well-prepared for the unexpected. With each adventure, you'll create lasting memories while maintaining the peace of mind that comes from being ready for anything. Take charge, be prepared, and let the wonders of the world unfold before you, secure in the knowledge that you're prepared to handle whatever comes your way!

Navigating Unfamiliar Environments - Embark on Safe Adventures

Welcome to the section on navigating unfamiliar environments, where we embark on a colorful journey through safety and awareness while exploring new horizons with your school-age children. As you venture into the unknown, it's important to equip yourselves with knowledge and strategies to ensure a secure and worry-free experience. In this section, we'll provide you with tips for researching local safety conditions, teaching children about basic safety rules, identifying child-friendly accommodations and transportation options, and implementing safety measures during outdoor activities and explorations.

Tips for Researching and Understanding Local Safety Conditions and Potential Hazards

Before diving headfirst into your adventures, take the time to research and understand the local safety conditions and potential hazards of your destination. Consult travel advisories, government websites, and reputable travel guides for up-to-date information. Learn about common safety concerns such as local laws, cultural norms, weather conditions, and any potential natural hazards. By equipping yourself with knowledge, you can make informed decisions and proactively mitigate potential risks.

Teaching Children about Basic Safety Rules and Awareness in Unfamiliar Surroundings

Empowering your children with basic safety rules and awareness is a vital aspect of navigating unfamiliar environments. Engage them in discussions about personal space, stranger danger, and how to identify and seek help from trusted authorities. Encourage them to be aware of their surroundings, stick together as a family, and follow your guidance. By fostering a culture of safety consciousness, you ensure that your children become active participants in their own well-being.

Identifying Child-Friendly Accommodations and Transportation Options

When exploring new destinations, it's essential to identify child-friendly accommodations and transportation options that prioritize safety and comfort. Look for hotels or vacation rentals that offer childproofing features, such as outlet covers and window locks. Consider locations with enclosed play areas or swimming pools with lifeguards. When it comes to transportation, choose reputable companies with child safety features like car seats or seat belts, and verify the availability of child-friendly transportation options such as strollers or baby carriers.

Implementing Safety Measures During Outdoor Activities and Exploring New Places

Outdoor activities and exploring new places are the heart of any family adventure. To ensure a safe and enjoyable experience, implement safety measures that suit the activities and environments you'll encounter. Dress appropriately for the weather and terrain, and equip yourselves with essential gear like sunscreen, insect repellent, and appropriate footwear. Establish boundaries for exploration, and communicate clear rules to children about staying together and seeking permission before venturing too far. Emphasize the importance of following trail markers, staying on designated paths, and respecting wildlife and nature. By proactively implementing safety measures, you create a secure environment for your family to embrace the wonders of the world.

As you navigate unfamiliar environments, remember that knowledge and awareness are your compass. Research local safety conditions, teach your children about basic safety rules, identify child-friendly accommodations and transportation options, and implement safety measures during outdoor activities. By prioritizing safety, you unlock the full potential of your family's adventures, creating treasured memories that will last a lifetime.

So, set forth with confidence and curiosity, knowing that you've prepared your family for a secure and awe-inspiring journey. Explore, discover, and marvel at the beauty of new horizons, while keeping safety and well-being at the forefront of your minds. Let the vibrant world unfold before you as you navigate unfamiliar environments with ease and peace of mind!

Ensuring Peace of Mind - Embrace the Journey with Confidence

Welcome to the section on ensuring peace of mind, where we embark on a vibrant exploration of strategies and tools to make your family's travel experience joyful, stress-free, and filled with wonder. As you set off on thrilling adventures with your school-age children, it's essential to cultivate a sense of tranquility and confidence. In this section, we'll delve into strategies for reducing travel-related stress and anxiety, staying informed about travel advisories and security updates, utilizing technology and apps for safety purposes, and fostering open communication and a positive travel mindset.

Strategies for Reducing Travel-Related Stress and Anxiety

Traveling can sometimes bring about stress and anxiety, especially when navigating unfamiliar territory. To counteract these feelings, incorporate strategies that promote relaxation and ease. Take breaks and allocate downtime to rest and rejuvenate. Practice deep breathing exercises or mindfulness techniques to center yourself amidst the excitement. Plan and organize your itinerary in advance, leaving room for flexibility. By implementing these strategies, you create a calming environment that allows you and your family to fully embrace the journey.

Staying Informed about Travel Advisories and Security Updates

Keeping abreast of travel advisories and security updates is crucial in ensuring a safe and worry-free adventure. Subscribe to official government travel websites or sign up for email alerts to receive the latest information about your destination. Stay informed about any potential risks, health advisories, or local security concerns. By staying updated, you can make informed decisions and take necessary precautions to protect your family.

Utilizing Technology and Apps for Safety Purposes

In the digital age, technology and apps offer a wealth of resources to enhance safety and peace of mind during your travels. Utilize mapping apps to navigate unfamiliar areas confidently. Download travel-specific apps that provide information on local emergency services, translation tools, or offline maps. Invest in a reliable mobile hotspot or data plan to stay connected and access information when needed. Embrace the power of technology as your trusty travel companion.

Encouraging Open Communication and Maintaining a Positive Travel Mindset

Open communication is a cornerstone of family travel. Encourage your children to share their thoughts, feelings, and concerns throughout the journey. Foster an environment where everyone's perspectives are valued. Maintain a positive travel mindset by focusing on the joy of discovery, creating shared memories, and embracing new experiences. Emphasize adaptability and resilience, knowing that challenges can be transformed into opportunities for growth. By fostering open communication and a positive mindset, you create an atmosphere of harmony, unity, and peace of mind.

As you embark on your family's travel adventure, remember that peace of mind is within your grasp. Implement strategies to reduce stress and anxiety, stay informed about travel advisories, utilize technology and apps for safety, and foster open communication and a positive travel mindset. With each step, you unlock the true essence of the journey, allowing your family to savor every moment with confidence, joy, and serenity.

So, set forth with a vibrant spirit and an unwavering sense of tranquility. Embrace the wonders of the world, secure in the knowledge that you've cultivated an environment of peace and confidence. Let the colors of the world paint your travel canvas, knowing that you've nurtured a journey filled with happiness, serenity, and unforgettable memories!

Chapter 12

Sustainable Travel - Making a Positive Impact

The Tripp family, known for their adventurous spirit, embarked on an exhilarating journey to Brazil to experience the vibrant and extravagant celebration of Carnivale. With their suitcases bursting with colorful costumes and excitement, they were ready to immerse themselves in the festive atmosphere.

As they arrived in Rio de Janeiro, the rhythmic beats of samba filled the air, setting the stage for an unforgettable adventure. The Tripp family, including Mr. and Mrs. Tripp and their three kids—Max, Dani, and Lucy—wasted no time in joining the lively street parades.

Dressed in their homemade, eye-catching costumes, they blended in seamlessly with the carnival-goers. Max rocked a sequined cape, Dani sported a feathered headdress, and Lucy twirled in a neon tutu that practically glowed in the dark.

As they joined a lively samba troupe, their lack of formal dance training became evident. But their enthusiasm more than compensated for any lack of skill. They swayed their hips, attempted samba steps, and laughed at their own dance floor mishaps.

It was during one particularly exuberant dance move that Mr. Tripp's cape got tangled with a fellow dancer's feathered costume, resulting in an impromptu "feather and sequin tango." The Tripp family and their accidental dance partner stumbled and spun around, their intertwined costumes creating a hilarious spectacle that had everyone around them cheering and applauding.

Not to be outdone by their parents, Max, Dani, and Lucy added their own comical flair to the festivities. Max, in an attempt to impress his siblings, tried a daring acrobatic move that ended with him unintentionally somersaulting into a foam-filled pool meant for the revelers. The crowd erupted in laughter as Max emerged from the foam, drenched but still wearing a broad grin.

Dani and Lucy, not to be outshined, joined a drumming group and attempted to keep the rhythm with their improvised tambourines. However, their enthusiasm sometimes got the best of them, and they would occasionally mix up the beats, creating a musical fusion that had both the drummers and the spectators in stitches.

Throughout the carnival festivities, the Tripp family embraced every moment with laughter and unabashed joy. They painted their faces, sampled traditional Brazilian street food, and danced with newfound friends until the sun began to rise.

As they bid farewell to the vibrant celebrations of Carnivale, the Tripp family carried with them not only memories of laughter and adventure but also a deeper appreciation for the power of celebration and embracing life's joyful moments. And while their dance moves may not have won them any awards, the Tripp family had certainly earned the title of the "Most Fun-Loving Family" at Carnivale.

Traveling with your school age kids gives you an opportunity to delve into the fascinating world of sustainable travel and explore how your family can make a positive impact on our planet. In this chapter, we will uncover the importance of sustainable travel, not only for the preservation of our beautiful world but also for the well-being of future generations. We will also discover ways to engage your children in environmental stewardship, fostering a sense of responsibility and care for the world around them.

Importance of Sustainable Travel:

When we embark on a journey, we become part of something greater than ourselves. Sustainable travel offers us an opportunity to contribute to the preservation of our planet and ensure a brighter future for our children. By embracing sustainable practices, we can minimize the negative environmental and social impacts caused by travel.

Preservation of the Planet for Future Generations:

Imagine a world where pristine forests are untouched, vibrant coral reefs thrive, and endangered species roam freely. Sustainable travel aims to protect and preserve these natural wonders, ensuring they remain intact for generations to come. By making conscious choices during our travels, we can help safeguard the delicate balance of ecosystems and promote the biodiversity that makes our planet so extraordinary.

Minimizing Negative Environmental and Social Impacts:

Traveling often leaves footprints, but we have the power to make them lighter. Sustainable travel seeks to minimize the negative impacts on the environment and local communities. By reducing waste, conserving energy, supporting responsible tourism practices, and respecting the cultural heritage of the places we visit, we can create a positive ripple effect and protect the very destinations we love to explore.

Engaging Children in Environmental Stewardship:

One of the most precious gifts we can give to our children is a sense of environmental stewardship. By involving them in sustainable travel practices, we empower them to become custodians of the Earth, nurturing a deep love and respect for nature. Travel becomes a transformative experience, instilling values of conservation, empathy, and responsibility in their young hearts.

Together, we will embark on a journey of discovery, where sustainable travel becomes an integral part of your family's adventures. We will explore eco-friendly destinations, uncover responsible tourism practices, and delve into engaging activities that ignite a sense of environmental stewardship in your children. Let us embark on this meaningful voyage, where every step we take becomes a positive contribution to the world we cherish.

Understanding Sustainable Travel

Welcome to the vibrant world of sustainable travel! In this section, we will dive into the colorful and captivating realm of sustainability, unraveling its essence and exploring the principles that guide this transformative way of exploring the world. Let's embark on a journey of understanding, where shades of green and blue paint a beautiful picture of responsible travel.

Definition of Sustainable Travel:

Sustainable travel, also known as eco-friendly or responsible travel, is a philosophy that harmonizes our wanderlust with the well-being of the planet and its inhabitants. It encompasses a mindful approach to exploring new horizons, where we strive to leave a positive impact on the environment, society, and culture of the destinations we visit. Sustainable travel is a kaleidoscope of choices, where each decision we make has the power to create a brighter future for our world.

Principles of Sustainable Travel:

Immerse yourself in the vibrant hues of sustainable travel, as we uncover the core principles that guide this transformative way of experiencing the world. Let's paint our canvas with these essential principles:

Conservation of Natural Resources:

Picture lush forests, crystal-clear rivers, and breathtaking landscapes teeming with life. The first principle of sustainable travel is the conservation of natural resources. It urges us to be mindful of our consumption, minimizing our impact on delicate ecosystems. By choosing eco-friendly transportation options, conserving water and energy, and supporting destinations that prioritize environmental protection, we contribute to the preservation of our planet's natural wonders.

Respect for Local Communities and Cultures:

Every corner of the globe boasts a unique tapestry of traditions, languages, and customs. The second principle of sustainable travel encourages us to embrace the rich diversity of local communities and cultures. As we explore new lands, we immerse ourselves in the vibrant colors of authenticity, respecting and valuing the traditions and heritage of the places we visit. By engaging in meaningful interactions with locals, supporting local businesses, and learning about their way of life, we promote cultural preservation and create bridges of understanding.

Minimization of Waste and Pollution:

Imagine a world where blue skies and pristine beaches remain untouched by pollution. The third principle of sustainable travel calls us to minimize waste and pollution, leaving behind only memories and footprints of positivity. We can embark on this colorful journey by adopting eco-friendly practices such as reducing single-use plastics, recycling whenever possible, and supporting businesses that prioritize sustainable waste management. Together, we can paint a cleaner and greener future for our world.

As you explore the chapters ahead, remember that sustainable travel is an invitation to embrace the vibrant palette of responsible choices. Each brushstroke contributes to the masterpiece of a healthier planet, leaving a legacy of inspiration for future generations. Let the colors of sustainability guide your family's travels, creating memories that shimmer with compassion, respect, and awe for the world around us.

Choosing Eco-Friendly Destinations

Prepare to embark on an exciting journey through a world of eco-friendly destinations, where vibrant landscapes and responsible practices blend harmoniously. In this section, we'll unveil a colorful palette of environmentally conscious travel options and highlight destinations that offer unique experiences for families with school-age children. Let's dive into a world of sustainability, where every shade brings us closer to the vibrant hues of responsible travel.

Researching Environmentally Conscious Destinations:

As you set out to plan your family's eco-friendly adventure, allow your imagination to soar as you explore destinations that prioritize sustainability. Consider these brushstrokes of information as you research environmentally conscious destinations:

1. Certifications and Eco-Labels to Look For:

Look out for certifications and eco-labels that signify a destination's commitment to sustainability. These symbols can guide you in choosing destinations that align with your values. Keep an eye out for labels such as Green Globe, EarthCheck, or the Global Sustainable Tourism Council

(GSTC) certification. These marks of distinction showcase destinations that have met rigorous sustainability criteria, assuring you of their eco-friendly practices.

2. Sustainable Tourism Initiatives in Different Regions:

Each region of the world paints its own canvas of sustainable tourism initiatives. Research and discover the innovative projects that are transforming destinations into beacons of sustainability. From community-led conservation efforts to renewable energy projects, these initiatives showcase the commitment of local communities and governments to preserving their natural and cultural heritage.

Highlighting Eco-Friendly Destinations Suitable for Families:

Prepare to be captivated by destinations that celebrate the magic of sustainability while offering enriching experiences for families with school-age children. Let's explore these vivid destinations and the unique experiences and attractions they have to offer:

1. Examples of Destinations with Sustainable Practices:

- Costa Rica: Immerse your family in the lush rainforests of Costa Rica, a beacon of sustainable tourism. Discover breathtaking biodiversity, participate in wildlife conservation programs, and explore eco-lodges nestled within nature reserves.

- Norway: Embark on a journey to the stunning fjords of Norway, where eco-friendly practices are deeply ingrained. Experience eco-friendly transportation options like electric ferries, go hiking amidst dramatic landscapes, and learn about renewable energy initiatives.

- Bhutan: Step into the mystical kingdom of Bhutan, known for its holistic approach to sustainability. Discover the country's commitment to Gross

National Happiness, explore pristine national parks, and engage in cultural exchanges with local communities.

Unique Experiences and Attractions Offered:

- Explore sustainable farms and organic food markets, where families can learn about sustainable agriculture and participate in farm-to-table experiences.

- Dive into marine conservation adventures, snorkeling or diving in coral reefs alongside marine biologists, and gaining a deeper understanding of the importance of protecting our oceans.

- Embark on guided nature walks and wildlife safaris, where expert guides educate families about the delicate ecosystems and conservation efforts taking place in the area.

Let the vibrant strokes of these eco-friendly destinations awaken the sense of wonder and curiosity in your children. Together, you'll embark on an adventure that fosters a love for nature, a respect for different cultures, and an appreciation for the positive impact of responsible travel. Remember, every destination holds a colorful story to tell, and by choosing eco-friendly options, you contribute to the masterpiece of a sustainable world for generations to come.

Responsible Tourism Practices for Families

Get ready to paint a vibrant picture of responsible tourism practices as we explore the colorful palette of sustainable choices for your family's travels. In this section, we'll dive into the brushstrokes of responsible transportation, eco-conscious accommodations, and sustainable dining options. Let's create a masterpiece of responsible tourism practices together, where each stroke of conscious decision-making contributes to a brighter future for our planet.

Sustainable Transportation Options:

Embark on a journey that leaves a lighter footprint on the world by considering these sustainable transportation options:

1. Choosing Eco-Friendly Modes of Transportation:

Embrace the vibrant hues of eco-friendly transportation as you plan your family's adventure. Opt for trains, buses, or bicycles whenever feasible, as they offer low carbon emissions and a chance to connect with the local surroundings. Choose public transportation, or consider electric or hybrid vehicles if a car is necessary. By taking these eco-conscious steps, you paint a greener path for your family's travels.

2. Tips for Minimizing Carbon Footprint While Traveling:

Add a splash of sustainability to your family's journey with these tips for minimizing your carbon footprint:

- Pack light: Lighter luggage reduces fuel consumption and greenhouse gas emissions during transportation.

- Offset your carbon emissions: Consider carbon offset programs that support environmental projects to counterbalance the emissions produced during your travels.

- Choose direct flights: Non-stop flights are more fuel-efficient than multiple layovers, reducing the overall carbon emissions of your journey.

Accommodation Choices:

Let's explore the spectrum of eco-conscious accommodations, where every brushstroke reflects a commitment to sustainability:

1. Eco-Lodges, Green Hotels, and Sustainable Resorts:

Experience a world where accommodation choices are a testament to environmental stewardship. Seek out eco-lodges, green hotels, or sustainable resorts that prioritize renewable energy, water conservation, waste management, and support for local communities. These vibrant accommodations offer an opportunity for your family to experience sustainability firsthand.

2. Staying in Locally-Owned Accommodations:

Immerse yourself in the vibrant culture and community of your destination by choosing locally-owned accommodations. These hidden gems often showcase sustainable practices and provide a deeper connection to the local environment. By supporting local businesses, you contribute to the preservation of the destination's unique charm.

Dining Sustainably:

Savor the flavors of responsible dining as we explore sustainable culinary experiences:

1. Supporting Local, Organic, and Sustainable Food Options:

Indulge in a gastronomic journey that celebrates local flavors and sustainable practices. Seek out restaurants and markets that prioritize local, organic, and sustainably sourced ingredients. By choosing these vibrant dining options, you support local farmers, reduce the carbon footprint of your meals, and encourage sustainable agricultural practices.

2. Minimizing Food Waste While Traveling:

Let's add a stroke of mindfulness to your family's dining experiences by minimizing food waste:

- Order consciously: Consider portion sizes and only order what you can consume to avoid food waste.

- Carry reusable containers: If leftovers are inevitable, bring reusable containers to store them for later enjoyment.

- Seek composting or food donation programs: Inquire with local establishments about their food waste management practices, supporting initiatives that reduce waste and benefit local communities.

With these responsible tourism practices, you paint a vivid and sustainable picture of your family's travels. Each brushstroke of conscious decision-making creates a brighter and more colorful future for our planet. Remember, every responsible choice brings us closer to a masterpiece of sustainability, where your family's adventures blend seamlessly with environmental stewardship.

Engaging Activities for Environmental Stewardship

Prepare for a vibrant and captivating section where we delve into the realm of engaging activities for environmental stewardship. Let's explore a colorful array of educational tours, volunteering opportunities, and eco-friendly outdoor adventures that will ignite a sense of wonder and inspire your family to become passionate advocates for the planet.

Educational Tours and Workshops:

Immerse yourselves in a world of knowledge and discovery through these engaging educational tours and workshops:

1. Nature Conservation Programs:

Embark on a captivating journey of nature conservation programs, where your family can actively participate in preserving the beauty of the natural world. Join hands-on initiatives such as tree planting, wildlife monitoring, or habitat restoration. These experiences provide invaluable lessons about the importance of environmental stewardship and empower your children to make a positive impact.

2. Environmental Learning Centers and Museums:

Unleash your curiosity and embrace the vivid tapestry of environmental learning centers and museums. Explore interactive exhibits that showcase the wonders of our planet, from diverse ecosystems to renewable energy innovations. Engage in workshops and demonstrations that teach sustainable practices, inspiring your family to become environmental champions.

Volunteering Opportunities:

Add vibrant brushstrokes of compassion and empathy to your family's travel experience through these volunteering opportunities:

1. Participating in Local Community Projects:

Immerse yourselves in the vibrant cultures of the destinations you visit by participating in local community projects. Engage in initiatives that support education, healthcare, or infrastructure development, providing valuable assistance to underserved communities. By fostering connections and contributing to local well-being, your family becomes a part of positive change.

2. Conservation Initiatives and Wildlife Rehabilitation Centers:

Ignite your family's passion for wildlife and conservation through volunteering at wildlife rehabilitation centers or engaging in conservation initiatives. Assist in the care of injured or orphaned animals, contribute to research efforts, and learn about the delicate balance of ecosystems. These hands-on experiences create lasting memories and instill a deep sense of responsibility towards protecting our planet's biodiversity.

Eco-Friendly Outdoor Adventures:

Step into a world of vibrant outdoor adventures that celebrate the beauty of nature and promote eco-consciousness:

Hiking, Biking, and Exploring Natural Landscapes:

Lace up your hiking boots, hop on your bikes, and embark on adventures through awe-inspiring natural landscapes. Traverse scenic trails, explore lush forests, and marvel at majestic mountains. These eco-friendly activities allow your family to connect with nature, promote physical well-being, and deepen your appreciation for the natural world.

Responsible Wildlife Encounters and Marine Conservation Activities:

Dive into the vibrant blues of responsible wildlife encounters and marine conservation activities. Seek out eco-conscious operators that prioritize the well-being and protection of animals. Engage in snorkeling or scuba diving adventures, where you can witness the beauty of coral reefs while learning about marine conservation efforts. These encounters foster respect for wildlife and inspire a sense of guardianship for our oceans.

With these engaging activities, your family becomes a vibrant force for environmental stewardship. Each adventure, workshop, and volunteer opportunity creates lasting impressions, nurturing a deep love and respect for our planet. Remember, every colorful stroke of engagement contributes to a masterpiece of sustainability, where your family's travel experiences become a catalyst for positive change.

Teaching Children about Sustainable Travel

Welcome to a colorful section dedicated to nurturing the environmental stewards of tomorrow—your children. Discover engaging and interactive ways to involve them in sustainable travel practices, where each stroke of knowledge and inspiration adds vibrant shades to their understanding of the world. Let's paint a picture of educational and enjoyable experiences that empower your children to become champions of sustainability.

Involving Children in Decision-Making:

Invite your children to take part in the decision-making process, giving them a voice in creating a sustainable travel experience. Let's explore two essential steps in involving children:

1. Discussing the Importance of Sustainable Choices:

Engage your children in conversations about sustainability and its significance. Explain the impact of our choices on the environment and communities. Discuss topics such as conservation, waste reduction, and cultural respect. By involving them in these discussions, you empower them to understand the importance of making sustainable choices.

2. Encouraging Responsible Behavior while Traveling:

Encourage your children to practice responsible behavior during their travels. Teach them to conserve resources, such as water and energy, by turning off lights and taps when not in use. Encourage them to dispose of waste properly and recycle whenever possible. By instilling these responsible habits, you foster their sense of environmental responsibility and contribute to a more sustainable future.

Fun and Interactive Ways to Learn about Sustainability:

Let creativity and curiosity take center stage as we explore colorful and engaging activities that bring sustainability to life:

1. Nature Scavenger Hunts and Eco-Challenges:

Ignite your children's sense of exploration through nature scavenger hunts and eco-challenges. Create colorful lists of items or eco-friendly tasks for them to complete, such as spotting specific plants or animals, collecting litter, or identifying sustainable practices. These activities immerse your children in the natural world and encourage them to observe and appreciate their surroundings.

2. Hands-On Activities and Eco-Crafts for Kids:

Unleash your children's creativity with hands-on activities and eco-crafts that celebrate sustainability. From creating recycled artwork to designing reusable shopping bags, these colorful projects empower your children to repurpose materials and reduce waste. Engage them in planting trees or starting a small vegetable garden, fostering their connection to the earth and teaching them the value of sustainable practices.

With these interactive experiences, your children become active participants in their own journey of environmental stewardship. Through discussions, responsible behavior, and engaging activities, you nurture a sense of responsibility and care for the world around them. Each stroke of knowledge and creativity adds vibrant shades to their understanding, cultivating a lifelong passion for sustainable travel and environmental well-being.

Remember, teaching children about sustainable travel is an opportunity to paint a brighter future for generations to come. Let their imaginations run wild and their hearts be filled with the colors of compassion and responsibility. Together, we inspire a new generation of environmental champions, adding vibrant strokes to the masterpiece of sustainable living.

Resources for Further Exploration

Prepare to embark on a journey of discovery beyond the pages of this travel guide, as we explore a vibrant palette of resources to deepen your family's understanding of sustainable travel. Let's uncover a trove of websites, books, documentaries, and local organizations that will inspire, educate, and guide you on your path towards a more sustainable future.

Dive into the boundless world of sustainable travel through these vibrant websites and online platforms:

- Sustainable Travel International (sustainabletravel.org): Discover a wealth of resources and information on sustainable travel practices, eco-friendly destinations, and community initiatives.

- Responsible Travel (responsibletravel.com): Uncover a colorful array of sustainable travel options and destinations, along with inspiring articles and tips for responsible tourism.

- The International Ecotourism Society (ecotourism.org): Immerse yourself in the world of ecotourism through their website, offering insights, research, and industry news to support sustainable travel practices.

Books and Documentaries for Children on Environmental Issues:

Ignite your children's curiosity and passion for the environment through these vibrant books and documentaries:

- "The Watcher: Jane Goodall's Life with the Chimps" by Jeanette Winter: This colorful picture book tells the inspiring story of Jane Goodall's dedication to chimpanzee research and conservation.

- "The Great Kapok Tree: A Tale of the Amazon Rainforest" by Lynne Cherry: Explore the vibrant Amazon rainforest through this beautifully illustrated book that highlights the importance of biodiversity and conservation.

- "Planet Earth" (TV series): Dive into the breathtaking world of nature through this captivating documentary series that showcases diverse ecosystems and the need for environmental preservation.

Local Organizations and Initiatives Supporting Sustainable Travel:

Immerse yourself in the vibrant tapestry of local organizations and initiatives dedicated to sustainable travel:

- Local Tourism Boards and Environmental Agencies: Connect with local tourism boards and environmental agencies of the destinations you plan to visit. They often provide valuable resources, eco-guides, and information on sustainable practices specific to the region.

- Community-Based Tourism Initiatives: Seek out community-based tourism initiatives that prioritize sustainable practices and support local communities. These initiatives offer authentic cultural experiences and a chance to contribute directly to local well-being.

- Environmental Conservation Groups: Engage with local environmental conservation groups that work tirelessly to protect and preserve natural and cultural heritage. They often provide opportunities for volunteer work, educational programs, and unique experiences that deepen your understanding of sustainability.

With these vibrant resources at your fingertips, your family can continue the colorful journey of sustainable travel long after your adventures have ended. Explore websites, delve into captivating books, watch documentaries, and connect with local organizations to expand your knowledge and make a positive impact. Let the knowledge you gain and the connections you make paint a brighter future for our planet, one brushstroke at a time.

Remember, the resources you explore become vivid hues on the canvas of your sustainable travel experience, enhancing your family's understanding and fostering a lifelong commitment to environmental stewardship.

Chapter 13

Creating Lasting Memories - Embracing the Joy of Family Travel

Well, we have arrived at the final destination of our travel guide—an exploration of the art of creating lasting memories and embracing the joy of family travel. As an educator and lifelong travel enthusiast, I have seen firsthand the transformative power of travel, particularly when it comes to building strong bonds and treasured memories within families. Now, it is time to reflect on the incredible journey we have taken together and discover ways to preserve these precious moments for years to come.

Throughout our travels, we have witnessed the wonder in our children's eyes as they discovered new landscapes, encountered different cultures, and embarked on thrilling adventures. These are the moments that define our family's narrative, and it is essential to find ways to capture and celebrate them.

One of the most popular and timeless methods of preserving memories is through the art of photography. As technology advances, it has become easier than ever to document our travels with high-quality cameras and smartphones. However, it is not just about capturing the perfect shot; it is about capturing the emotions, the laughter, and the shared experiences that make each trip unique. Take the time to experiment with different angles, compositions, and lighting to convey the essence of your family's adventures.

In addition to photography, consider creating a travel journal that acts as a tangible keepsake. Encourage your children to write about their experiences, sketch their favorite landmarks, or even collect small mementos like ticket stubs or pressed flowers. By involving them in the process, you not only foster their creativity but also empower them to actively participate in preserving their own memories.

As you gather these visual and written treasures, don't let them languish on hard drives or hidden in drawers. Instead, create physical albums or digital presentations that you can revisit together as a family. These collections will become cherished time capsules, transporting you back to the sights, sounds, and emotions of your past adventures. Whether it's a cozy evening at home or a gathering with extended family and friends, these visual narratives will ignite conversations, spark laughter, and remind everyone of the incredible moments you shared together.

Beyond the traditional methods of preserving memories, consider exploring new and innovative ways to celebrate your family's travels. In the age of social media, you may choose to share snippets of your journey with friends and family around the world. Create a dedicated travel blog or use platforms like Instagram to showcase your favorite moments, inspiring others to embark on their own adventures. This not only serves as a virtual scrapbook but also creates a supportive community of fellow travelers who can share their own tips and experiences.

Remember, it's not just about the final destination or ticking off items from a bucket list; it's about the journey itself—the moments of discovery, the laughter, and the bonding that happens along the way. Family travel is an investment in creating memories that will last a lifetime, and by embracing the joy of the experience, you can strengthen the connections within your family and foster a sense of wonder and curiosity in your children.

As we conclude this travel guide, I want to express my heartfelt gratitude for accompanying me on this journey. I hope these chapters have provided you with inspiration, practical advice, and a sense of excitement for the possibilities that lie ahead. Remember, the world is your playground, and with each adventure, you are not only shaping your children's lives but also creating a tapestry of shared memories that will endure.

So, go forth, explore, and embrace the joy of family travel. Cherish every moment, capture the magic, and hold onto these experiences with all your heart. Your family's story is unique and beautiful, and by documenting and preserving your adventures, you are ensuring that the spirit of travel will live on in your lives for generations to come.

Safe travels and may your future journeys be filled with laughter, love, and boundless discovery. Bon voyage!

About the Author

Alice Evans is a teacher, counselor, and a seasoned mother of three. With a passion for exploring the world and a deep understanding of child development, Alice has embarked on countless travel adventures with her own children. From the early stages of juggling strollers and bottles to navigating the ever-changing needs of toddlers and beyond, she has experienced the joys and challenges of traveling with kids firsthand.

As an experienced educator and counselor, Alice brings her expertise in child psychology and her nurturing nature to the forefront of her writing. Through her books, she offers invaluable insights, practical tips, and heartfelt anecdotes that resonate with parents looking to create meaningful travel experiences for their families.

With Alice's warm and witty writing style, she effortlessly guides readers through the triumphs and tribulations of family travel, emphasizing the importance of connection, cultural sensitivity, and personal growth along the way. Her relatable stories and expert advice inspire parents to embrace the transformative power of travel, fostering a sense of curiosity, resilience, and togetherness within their own families.

When she's not traveling or writing, Alice can be found teaching and counseling children, passionately advocating for the benefits of exploring the world and creating lasting memories with loved ones. She continues to inspire families around the globe to embark on their own unforgettable journeys, one adventure at a time.

Printed in Great Britain
by Amazon

30238962R00116